The
Essentials

AN ORTHODOX CHRISTIAN CATECHISM

**+ARCHPRIEST PAVEL SOUCEK
EDITED BY FATHER JOHN UDICS**

ANCIENT FAITH PUBLISHING
CHESTERTON, INDIANA

The Essentials: An Orthodox Christian Catechism
Copyright © 2026 Jacob Soucek

All rights reserved. No part of this publication may be reproduced by any means, electronic, mechanical, photocopying, recording, scanning, or otherwise, without the prior written permission of the publisher.

Published by:
Ancient Faith Publishing
A Division of Ancient Faith Ministries
1050 Broadway, Suite 6
Chesterton, IN 46304

All Old Testament quotations, unless otherwise identified, are from the Orthodox Study Bible, © 2008 by St. Athanasius Academy of Orthodox Theology (published by Thomas Nelson, Inc., Nashville, Tennessee) and are used by permission. New Testament quotations are from the New King James Version of the Bible, © 1982 by Thomas Nelson, Inc., and are used by permission.

Cover art by Fr. Pavel Soucek, based on a 17th century Eastern European church; cover design by Sophie Ries

ISBN: 978-1-955890-97-7

Library of Congress Control Number: 2026930535

CONTENTS

Foreword	vii
Note from the Editors	xi
CHAPTER 1: *The Symbol of the Orthodox Faith—The Creed*	1
A Brief Explanation of the Creed	2
CHAPTER 2: *The Ten Commandments of God*	23
CHAPTER 3: *Christ's Twofold Commandment of Love*	31
CHAPTER 4: *The Holy Sacraments*	35
Baptism	36
Chrismation	38
The Eucharist	40
Confession	42

The Priesthood (Holy Orders)	44
Marriage (Holy Matrimony)	48
Unction (the Sacrament of Healing)	52

CHAPTER 5: *The Bible and Holy Tradition* — 57
   The Bible — 57
   Holy Tradition — 61
   The Seven Ecumenical Councils — 62

CHAPTER 6: *The Orthodox Services and Liturgical Cycles* — 65

CHAPTER 7: *The Twelve Great Feasts* — 71
   The Entrance of Our Lord Jesus Christ into Jerusalem (Palm Sunday) — 71
   The Ascension of Our Lord and Savior Jesus Christ — 73
   The Descent of the Holy Spirit (Pentecost Sunday), The Feast of the Most Holy Trinity — 74
   The Nativity of the Most Holy Theotokos — 75
   The Universal Exaltation (Elevation) of the Life-Giving Cross — 77
   The Entrance (Presentation) of the Theotokos into the Temple — 78
   The Nativity According to the Flesh of Our Lord and God and Savior Jesus Christ — 79

Contents

The Theophany (Epiphany) of Our Lord Jesus Christ	81
The Meeting (Presentation) of Our Lord in the Temple	83
The Annunciation of the Most Holy Theotokos	84
The Transfiguration of Our Lord Jesus Christ	86
The Falling Asleep (Dormition) of the Most Holy Theotokos	87
Major Feasts	89

CHAPTER 8: *The Paschal Liturgical Cycle* — 91

CHAPTER 9: *The Orthodox Divine Liturgies* — 103
    The Divine Liturgy of St. John Chrysostom — 106
    The Divine Liturgy of St. Basil the Great — 106
    The Divine Liturgy of St. James — 107
    The Divine Liturgy of the Presanctified Gifts — 107

CHAPTER 10: *Fasting and Praying* — 111

CHAPTER 11: *The Trisagion Prayers* — 119

About the Author — 123
For Further Reading — 127

Foreword

It is both a privilege and a profound personal joy to write this foreword for my father's work. Father Pavel Soucek was not only a devoted priest and scholar but also a man whose life bore constant witness to the power of faith, perseverance, and truth. For those who knew him, his wisdom and unwavering love for God were the marks of a soul entirely given to the service of Christ and His Church.

Growing up, I saw firsthand the depth of his conviction and the sincerity of his calling. Faith was not, for him, a mere intellectual pursuit but was how he lived his life. Whether he was studying Scripture, preparing sermons, or patiently answering the questions of those new to the Faith, my father's heart was always turned toward one goal: to help others encounter the living truth of God through the Orthodox Church.

His journey was far from easy. From his youth in communist Czechoslovakia, where the open practice of faith came with real risk, to his years of theological searching in the West, my father's path was marked by sacrifice and steadfast courage. He sought not comfort, but truth. And when he found that truth in the Orthodox Faith, he embraced it with the same humility and joy that characterized every aspect of his priesthood.

This book—*The Essentials: An Orthodox Christian Catechism*—is in many ways the culmination of his life's work. It is written not only for theologians or scholars but for all who hunger to understand what it means to live as an Orthodox Christian. Every page reflects his pastoral heart and his desire to make the profound truths of the Faith understandable, practical, and alive.

For those who read these words today, know that you are holding something deeply personal: not just a book but a reflection of my father's soul. His life was a living catechism—rooted in prayer, illuminated by study, and expressed through love.

Foreword

Artwork by Fr. Pavel Soucek

May this work continue to guide seekers, strengthen believers, and remind us all that truth, when sought with humility and faith, will always lead us home—to Christ.

May his memory be eternal.

—Jacob Soucek
Son of Archpriest Pavel Soucek

Note from the Editors

WHEN +FR. PAVEL SOUCEK COMPLETED this work in 1999, many differences existed in liturgical practices within the various ethnic and cultural communities that make up the Orthodox Church worldwide. During his pastoral ministry, Fr. Pavel served a number of parishes in the Orthodox Church of America (OCA) and, as such, his book is oriented to the traditions of that jurisdiction, which has its roots in Russian and Slavic Orthodoxy. In preparing this little book for publication, we recognized that our readership today is heavily pan-Orthodox and includes many converts and inquirers into the Faith who encompass various jurisdictions and cultural traditions within Orthodoxy. Accordingly, we have attempted to present a version of this catechism that can be understood by members of any Orthodox parish regardless of jurisdiction or location.

The primary purpose of this book is to emphasize the *basics* of Orthodox Christianity, and it is simply not possible to cover all of the different practices and traditions that still exist between and amongst Orthodox jurisdictions and dioceses down to individual churches at the parish level. We feel we have done our best to present these differences (where necessary) as we understand them, while remaining true to Fr. Pavel's intended message.

Most importantly, we ask our readers to dwell on the one essential truth that clearly shines forth in this work and in Fr. Pavel's life, that the fundamental beliefs, teachings, and worldview of the Orthodox Faith have remained unchanged over the Church's two thousand–plus year history.

CHAPTER 1

The Symbol of the Orthodox Faith—The Creed

I believe in one God, the Father Almighty, Maker of Heaven and Earth and of all things visible and invisible.

And in one Lord Jesus Christ, the Son of God, the only-begotten, begotten of the Father before all ages. Light of light; true God of true God; begotten, not made; of one essence with the Father; by Whom all things were made; Who for us men and for our salvation came down from Heaven, and was incarnate of the Holy Spirit and the Virgin Mary, and became man. And He was crucified for us under Pontius Pilate, and suffered, and was buried. And the third day He arose again, according to the Scriptures, and ascended into Heaven, and sits at the right hand of the Father; and He shall come again with glory to judge the living and the dead; Whose Kingdom shall have no end.

And in the Holy Spirit, the Lord, the Giver of Life, Who proceeds from the Father; Who with the Father and the Son together is worshipped and glorified; Who spoke by the prophets.

In one Holy, Catholic, and Apostolic Church. I acknowledge one baptism for the remission of sins. I look for the resurrection of the dead and the life of the world to come. Amen.[1]

A Brief Explanation of the Creed

I believe in one God, the Father Almighty, Maker of Heaven and Earth and of all things visible and invisible

---

1   https://www.oca.org/orthodoxy/prayers/symbol-of-faith.

There is only one God. He is truly our heavenly Father for He gives us life, cares and provides for us, teaches us, guides and protects us, and limitlessly loves us. Because we all are His sons and daughters, He gives us, as our inheritance, His heavenly Kingdom.

This one and only God exists in three Divine Persons: the Father, the Son, and the Holy Spirit. This is the Most Holy Trinity. Each Divine Person is an individual yet, being one God, they cannot be divided. And each has, in fullness, the very same Divinity and all the qualities and attributes of that Divinity. Whatever one Person is, the other two are also. Whatever one has, the other two have as well. Where one is, there are the other two. There are three Divine Persons, but not three Gods, only one. This, of course, cannot be grasped with our minds.

It is not possible to list all God's attributes. He is almighty because He does whatever He pleases. There is nothing He cannot do. He is eternal for He has no beginning and no end in His existence. There never was a moment when God did not exist. He is all-knowing, for He knows everything there is to know in the past, present, and future. He is everywhere present because, not being limited by time or space, He is everywhere at the very same moment. God is pure spirit and He creates by mere thought.

God created absolutely everything that is in existence. Even though many things seem to be man-made, it is God who created that person and gave him or her the ability to form and fashion various things. He also created countless things that we cannot see. This is so because of great distances in space or because they are of a spiritual nature and cannot be captured by our physical sight. These include spiritual creatures, for example, such as the holy angels.

God created human beings according to His own image and likeness, with an immortal soul, a mind, and a body. He also granted us the wonderful but dangerous gift of free will, which He also gave to His angels.

And in one Lord Jesus Christ, the Son of God, the only-begotten, begotten of the Father before all ages. Light of light; true God of true God; begotten, not made; of one essence with the Father; by Whom all things were made

God is the sovereign Lord of the whole universe. Therefore, each Divine Person of the Most Holy Trinity is the Lord.

The Lord Jesus Christ is the Divine Son, the only begotten Son. The relationship between God the Father and God the Son is truly divine and cannot be understood by humans. Therefore, if we say that the Son is begotten of the Father, there is no time or specific time-point involved. True, the Son is generated by the Father, but this has an eternal character—that is, as the Father is eternal, without beginning, so is the Son. Simply, God the Son was always in existence. Like God the Father, He was not made or created. Within time, when He was born in Bethlehem, He also became man, keeping His divinity without any alteration. Thus, Jesus is God the Son from eternity and the Son of Man from a certain point in time.

As the opposite to the darkness of evil, God is spoken of as the life-giving Light. That is why we say that Jesus, the Son of God, being God Himself is also of Light and of the true God. The Son is in absolute totality what the Father is.

When God created the universe, all of the Trinity was in a creative action. Thus we say, speaking about the Son of God, that the Father, the Creator, made everything through Him.

Who for us men and for our salvation came down from Heaven, and was incarnate of the Holy Spirit and the Virgin Mary, and became man

The Son of God voluntarily left the beauty and the bliss of heaven and descended to earth. He further lowered Himself by becoming one of us, a human. We say that in doing this, He emptied Himself. His taking upon Himself our human body, the Incarnation or enfleshment, was accomplished by the power of the Holy Spirit who overshadowed the Blessed Virgin Mary, who then gave birth to Jesus Christ. The Virgin Mary remained a virgin before, during, and after our Lord's birth in the flesh.

Jesus became a perfect man, having everything in common with us except sinfulness. Simultaneously, He remained the perfect God, for He never gave up His divinity. Therefore, in the one Person of Jesus Christ there are two natures: the divine and the human. These two natures are clearly distinguishable. They are not mixed, yet they are inseparable. The Virgin Mary gave birth exactly to this one Person, Jesus Christ our Lord. Therefore, she is correctly called the Mother of God.

Our Lord Jesus came to us for our salvation. He took upon Himself the sins of humankind from the very beginning of its existence to the end of time in order to restore the whole of creation to its original beauty. He came to win us over from death and devilish destruction, breaking the bondage of sin. He is the only true Savior, the Messiah as announced by the prophets.

And He was crucified for us under Pontius Pilate, and suffered, and was buried

Our Lord Jesus Christ redeems the world through His suffering and death on the Cross. He was not forced to do this. He suffered and died for us out of His limitless love for humankind and He did it completely voluntarily.

Christ came to reopen the doors of Paradise, which were closed because Adam and Eve had disobeyed God. Their sin affected the whole of humankind for all ages. However, it is not guilt that we would inherit and be born with because of the sin of our first parents, as the Western Church erroneously teaches. What we inherit from Adam and Eve's error is the aftereffect of their sinful action: estrangement from God through our nature, which had become twisted, and the inclination to sin. The divine image and likeness—according to which God originally created us—became blurred and dimmed, and the gates to the heavenly Kingdom were closed.

In His infinite wisdom and kindness, Jesus also revealed to us, as His continuing saving act, the Way of returning to God—for we all in our sinfulness are always ready to walk away from God and miss the target. This revealed Way is Jesus Christ Himself; for to follow Him staunchly means to walk toward our personal salvation. To be a Christian is to be a follower of Christ.

And the third day He arose again, according to the Scriptures

During His three-day burial, our Lord Jesus was at several places at the same time. "In the tomb with the body and in hell with the soul, in paradise with the thief and on the throne with the Father and the Spirit, wast Thou, O boundless Christ, filling all things."[2]

On the third day, our Savior Jesus Christ, out of His own divine power, rose from the dead. This most glorious event, as recorded in Holy Scripture, perfectly confirms the truthfulness of Christ's revelation and the absolute correctness of our Faith. Without Christ's Resurrection, as the Apostle Paul states, our Faith would be in vain.

And ascended into Heaven, and sits at the right hand of the Father

After His Resurrection, Jesus spent over a month and a half with His apostles and disciples, further teaching and instructing them. Then He

---

2   From the prayer of the priest at the Great Entrance, Divine Liturgy of St. John Chrysostom.

left the earth and ascended into heaven where He assumed His position as one of the Most Holy Trinity. But even then, His human nature was not dissolved or annihilated. Our Lord Jesus is in heaven with His glorified human body.

And He shall come again with glory to judge the living and the dead; Whose Kingdom shall have no end

Jesus Christ promised to return again at the end of time. When this will be, no one knows but God Himself. Jesus advised us to be watchful and ready every day for His Return. It will happen suddenly and unexpectedly.

When Our Lord Jesus comes again, He will gather all the human beings from the very beginning of Creation, dead or still living at that time, and He will judge each and every one of us according to our deeds.

After this is completed, Satan and his hordes will be ultimately defeated. They will be sent forever with all those who follow them to the place of no return, the place of eternal damnation and torment.

The faithful will enter the place of maximal joy and beauty: Paradise, the heavenly Jerusalem, God's Kingdom, and they will live there forever.

And in the Holy Spirit, the Lord, the Giver of Life, Who proceeds from the Father; Who with the Father and the Son together is worshipped and glorified; Who spoke by the prophets

The Holy Spirit is one of the most Holy Trinity, God the Lord. Christ called Him the Comforter, the Spirit of Truth.

As the body must have a soul in order to live, so the life of the whole cosmos, but above all, the life of the Church, depends on the presence of the Holy Spirit. He indeed is the Giver of Life.

As the Father and the Son are eternal, so is the Holy Spirit. As they are uncreated, so is the Holy Spirit. The existence of the Son was defined as being "begotten." The existence of the Holy Spirit as "proceeding," proceeding from the Father only, not from the Son as the Western Church erroneously teaches. This procession from the Father is again eternal, as is the Son's being begotten.

Therefore, these terms are infinitely more complex and mysterious than their dictionary explanations, and the human mind simply cannot grasp them.

Our worship belongs to God exclusively. Therefore, we worship the Father and the Son and the Holy Spirit, for they are the three Divine Persons, the Most Holy Trinity, One God.

It was the Holy Spirit who inspired the prophets of old. It was the Holy Spirit who filled the apostles with courage and wisdom and inspired the evangelists to the correct recording of Christ's life and teaching. It was the Holy Spirit who protected the Holy Fathers of the ecumenical councils from making any erroneous decisions and proclamations. It is the Holy Spirit who spoke and speaks through all these people for our edification, sanctification, and salvation: apostles, prophets, preachers, evangelists, confessors, martyrs, ascetic fathers and mothers, and every righteous soul made perfect in the Faith.

In one Holy, Catholic, and Apostolic Church

As God is one, the Church is one. Any division in and of the Church is unacceptable, for it is offensive to God, who is One. The true Church is of divine origin, and therefore any man-made factions, sects, and denominations cannot be true churches. There is only one truth, one correct theology, one correct worship, and that is exactly what the word *Orthodoxy* means.

The reuniting of the other churches with the true Church—the Orthodox Christian Church—cannot be accomplished on the basis of false ecumenism, that is, ecumenism based on compromise. Reunion of the churches can only happen through the power of the Holy Spirit, who will enlighten the non-Orthodox, bringing them into the Orthodox Church. We all need to pray intensively for this unity.

The Church is holy, not because of us, obviously, but because God is holy. He is the One who established the Church and fills her with His holiness. However, He invites us and gives to all of us the abundance of grace to enter into the holy way of life. Christ said that we should become holy as is our heavenly Father.

The Church is catholic because she possesses the fullness of divine doctrine and of spiritual treasures. These are then available to literally everyone, but not on the terms of those who desire them, rather on the terms of the Church, of God Himself. This catholicity of the Church goes far beyond a mere universality.

The Church is apostolic for she adheres, with no compromise, to the teachings of Christ as the holy apostles preached them. Therefore, the Church's apostolicity cannot be understood as a kind of illusive lifeless continuum. The Church is apostolic because the apostolic teaching is very much alive in her.

The Church is also hierarchical. She is governed by God Himself. Both the clergy and the laity are absolutely essential for the Church's existence. They both must accept God's revelation and His leadership completely and without exceptions. They are both fully responsible to God. They both have one goal, one zeal, one direction, and one work in the Church. But each has a different level of authority that must be respected and not fought against. At the same time, in God's eyes, no one is more or less important than another. The Church is the Body of Christ. Christ is beautiful, and His Body, the Church, must be kept beautiful.

There are a number of national, autonomous, and autocephalous Orthodox churches. But the emphasis is on *Orthodox*. Each of them might have some specific national and/or administrative characteristics and customs, but these do not and cannot interfere with their Orthodoxy. They are of the same Orthodox doctrine and worship, holding to the same Holy Tradition.

The Orthodox Church is conciliar. This means that other than Jesus Christ, the Church has no centralized power in one man. She has nothing even remotely resembling the Western Church's papacy. Our holy patriarchs are bishops of the same power and responsibilities; they are equal to each other. The Patriarch of Constantinople is first among equals and his position is one of honor. He, as the other patriarchs, has no authority to make decisions on his own that would bind all the Church everywhere. On certain aspects of

Church life, the patriarchs make their decisions corporately and unanimously. For certain regions, regional councils are called together to make decisions. But the highest authority in the Orthodox Church is the ecumenical council—the highest authority on earth. We have the decisions of the seven ecumenical councils, which are binding on all Orthodox Christians everywhere. The last of these councils was the Seventh Ecumenical Council, convened in Nicaea in 787. There has been no ecumenical council since, but this does not mean that there cannot be others in the future, if needed.

On the level of the autocephalous (self-governing) churches, decisions are made by the council of bishops, presided over by the metropolitan archbishop. This council is called the Holy Synod of Bishops. Each of the councils—regional and ecumenical—and Holy Synods, are guided by the Holy Spirit who leads the participants to make correct decisions.

The Church is also timeless, in that she does not undergo any radical changes in the course of time. Naturally, in different periods, the Church must face various new issues and challenges. But the solutions to these issues must always be based strictly on Holy Scripture and Orthodox Holy Tradition and not on the introduction of novelties that are incompatible with Church doctrine and spirituality.

The Church in heaven is called victorious, for those living eternally in the Kingdom already have won their crown and enjoy the fruits of their earthly efforts as Christians. The Church on earth is called militant, because we are still in a spiritual war against all that would take us away from our goal, which is to reach Paradise with honor.

I acknowledge one baptism for the remission of sins

Through the Sacrament of Holy Baptism, we are received into communion with Christ and become members of His Holy Church.

The remission of sin by the administering of this sacrament addresses not only the adult person but the innocent baby as well, because it indicates a total change of the baptized person, regardless of age. In Baptism, we die to the sinful world and are transferred into sinless communion with Christ. With our Lord we die, and with Him we are resurrected. We are not anymore *of* this world, only *in* it.

The Sacrament of Holy Baptism is not repeatable, as are, for example, the Sacraments of Confession and Holy Communion. There is only one Baptism, and it enables us to make use of the other Sacraments so that we can constantly keep renewing the spotless robe of incorruption given to us at Baptism. It gives us the chance to live the life of an Orthodox Christian in total sincerity.

I look for the resurrection of the dead

A human being is a unique union of body, mind, and soul. God had no intention to ever distort this unity, but through sin, death entered into the lives of men and women. The physical body cannot live without the soul, and when the soul separates from the body, physical death occurs.

The soul, on the other hand, is immortal. It cannot die and has no difficulty continuing its existence even after the death of the body, for it does not need any sustenance in the form of food, drink, sleep, rest and so on. Even though bodily death is only temporary, this division of the soul and body clearly manifests the destructive power of all evil that works fiercely against the will of God.

When the dead body is buried in the ground, it awaits the day of the Last Judgment. The separated soul awaits Judgment Day either in heaven or in hell, according to the preliminary judgment that takes place immediately after the soul departs from the body. Because this preliminary judgment is not final, we continue to pray for departed souls without distinguishing whether they might be in heaven or in hell. The Orthodox Church has never held to a doctrine of purgatory or limbo.

The Church teaches that at the Last Day Christ will resurrect our reposed bodies, and our bodies will receive an existential quality suitable for life in the eternal realm. While this is one of the profound mysteries of the Faith, about which we know little, we believe that at the Second Coming the wholeness of each human person is restored. We refer to this as the glorification of the resurrected body: The same soul unites with the same body as they were before they were separated at the time of death.

The decision Christ makes at the Last and universal Judgment will be final and definite. Those people who were good will enter the heavenly Kingdom for joyful, everlasting life. Those people who were evil will be sent to eternal punishment in hell.

And the life of the world to come. Amen

No one knows where Paradise is and what it looks like. For that matter, no one knows what hell is like. The holy Apostle Paul was granted the privilege to see, for a brief period of time, the beauty of heaven. He found it impossible to describe. He said that no one has ever seen, heard, or imagined the beauty God has prepared for those who love Him.

The Orthodox Church has never taught the total destruction of the earth and the whole universe at the end of time, and consequently, never adhered to the teaching of the so-called "second creation."[3] To the contrary, the Church looks forward to the world to come, which is this world that

---

3 The theory that God will eliminate all suffering, death, and pain at the end of time, as He remakes the heavens

God created. This world will not first be destroyed or annihilated but will be changed and made anew, and it will be immensely more beautiful. All of creation will rejoice in the new Paradise, glorifying God forever. Amen.

The truths of the Creed were formulated, not invented, by the Holy Fathers of the First Ecumenical Council in Nicaea (AD 325) and the Second Ecumenical Council in Constantinople (AD 381). Although the actual title is the Nicene-Constantinopolitan Creed, in common usage the faithful refer to it as simply the Creed or the Nicene Creed. Notwithstanding, every Orthodox Christian should know the Creed from memory and be able to offer a brief explanation of its history and meaning.

---

and the earth. This will be an eternal period of peace and renewal on earth through the New Jerusalem.

CHAPTER 2

The Ten Commandments of God

THE TEN COMMANDMENTS (Ex. 20:1–17) were divinely inscribed on two tablets of stone and given to our holy forefather Moses on Mount Sinai by God Himself.

They never did and never will become "out of fashion." They are valid now as then and unto the end of time.

I am the Lord your God. . . . You shall have no other gods before Me

Only pagans believe in many gods. We are commanded to believe in the one true God and in Him only.

The Holy Orthodox Church precisely records and teaches God's revelation. He revealed Himself to us as one God in the Holy Trinity: the Father, the Son, and the Holy Spirit.

You shall not make for yourself an idol or a likeness of anything in heaven above, or in the earth beneath, or in the waters under the earth. You shall not bow down to them or serve them

God is absolutely clear that making statues or pictures of anything from the created world in order to establish them as deities, and to worship and serve them, is not only forbidden, with no exception, but is intolerably insulting to the true God, who is the Creator of all those things these idols would depict. This includes worshiping kings as gods, as was the custom in ancient times.

The holy icons of the Orthodox Church do not belong in this category because a) they are not idols but spiritual images of the prototypes living in the heavenly realm and thus, through them, the one and true God is glorified; b) the holy icons are not worshipped, for worship belongs to God exclusively, but they are merely venerated, respected;

c) we do not venerate the materials from which the icons are made, but we venerate God's angels, saints, and holy events depicted on icons; d) we do not serve the icons, but quite to the contrary, they serve us because they educate us, take their place in liturgical celebrations, lead us to prayer, uplift us spiritually, and stress the truths of the Holy Scriptures and Holy Tradition.

You shall not take the name of the Lord your God in vain

The name of God is absolutely sacred. Invoking God's Name is a prayer and can be nothing else. Any other use of His Name is a serious insult to Him. The Third Commandment reminds us to take great care, even during our personal prayers, to avoid any mindless, careless, or strictly mechanical use of God's Name.

Remember the Sabbath Day, to keep it holy. Six days you shall labor and do all your work, but the seventh day is the Sabbath of the Lord your God

For us Christians, Sunday is the Sabbath. Sunday is appropriately called the Lord's Day.

On Sunday, much work ceases and we direct our thoughts and deeds to God. The greatest highlight of this day is the worship we offer to God at the Divine Liturgy in His holy temple and our reception of the life-giving Sacrament of His precious Body and Blood. There is seldom a valid excuse that would prevent us from doing so.

We respect the great feast days throughout the year in the same way we respect Sundays. Each Sunday and festal celebration starts on the preceding evening with Vespers or the Vigil service.

Honor your father and your mother that it may be well with you, and your days may be long upon the good land the Lord your God is giving to you

Love, respect, honor, and mutual understanding are absolutely essential for peaceful family relationships. God finds it so important that He promises even earthly rewards to all who faithfully keep this Commandment, that is, good health and long life. Such behavior is then extended in society to our teachers and to civil authorities. But above all, we love, respect, and honor the spiritual leaders of the Church.

The Ten Commandments of God

You shall not murder

We did not create; we should not destroy. Only the Lord our God, who is the giver of life, has unlimited power over His creation. So-called "mercy killing," assisted suicide, abortion, or the death penalty are absolutely unthinkable for the Orthodox Christian. We cannot agree with these things, support them, or become in any way part of them. Obviously murder, rape, abuse, fighting, harming ourselves or others, and so on are part of this commandment as well. Killing animals for sport or entertainment, or harming or abusing them also falls under this commandment.

Refusing to take care of ourselves or others in sickness, when there is reasonable hope for recovery, is covered by this commandment as well. This commandment also includes the "killing" of the good name of our neighbor by gossip and slander, and causing psychological or spiritual harm to others.

You shall not commit adultery

Sex has God's blessing when it is kept between husband and wife. Any violation of this establishment is considered a destruction of the sacramental union granted in the Sacrament of Matrimony and a misusing of a wonderful gift of God.

You shall not steal

Every Christian willingly and gladly shares his or her worldly possessions with those in need. On the other hand, deliberately taking anything from others, no matter how small or insignificant the object, is stealing. If a person steals something, they must repent and return the object to the rightful owner or pay for it.

You shall not bear false witness against your neighbor

Orthodox Christians do not lie because we believe in God, who Himself is absolute Truth. If we lie, our faith also becomes a lie. If we lie or gossip about our neighbor or slander him or her, such lies can easily "kill" the neighbor's good name. Then, of course, we also violate the Sixth Commandment. All who gladly listen to such lies, believe them, or spread them around are violating this commandment as well.

You shall not covet your neighbor's wife . . . or whatever belongs to your neighbor

If we desire our neighbor's wife, we have already committed adultery in our mind, which is explicitly against the Seventh Commandment.

As for our neighbor's possessions, our desire for them has its ground in greed and envy. Rather, whatever our neighbor possesses, might it be material things, talents, authority, position in society, success and so on, we should give thanks to God that He so wonderfully rewarded our neighbor. We should also keep on thanking God for whatever He gives us and be fully content, even if it seems to us not to be much. Any deliberate destructive action against our neighbor's possessions, or even only a destructive wish, greatly violates this commandment.

CHAPTER 3

Christ's Twofold Commandment of Love

THIS COMMANDMENT IS CALLED, IN the Gospels, "the great commandment." It is also referred to as the two commandments of love or the new commandment. In the Holy Gospel according to St. Matthew, it is written: "Jesus said . . . 'You shall love the LORD your God with all your heart, with all your soul, and with all your mind.' This is the first and great commandment. And the second is like it: 'You shall love your neighbor as yourself.' On these two commandments hang all the Law and the Prophets" (22:37–40).

THE ESSENTIALS

Artwork by Fr. Pavel Soucek

This does not mean that the Ten Commandments of old are being canceled. Rather, they are being elevated from the level of the fear of punishment to the level of love, which expects nothing but gives everything.

Love here has nothing to do with sentimental sobbing or unstable emotional outbursts. This is heroic love, which is ready at any moment to give up everything, including life, for God, and in the name of God, for the neighbor as well.

Our Lord Jesus Christ Himself gave us an absolutely perfect example of such love. If we understand that to be Christian is to be Christ's follower in everything, then we also understand that ignoring this greatest commandment excludes us from Christ's flock. It is love that shows we belong to Christ.

CHAPTER 4

The Holy Sacraments

THE SACRAMENTS ARE ALSO CALLED Mysteries. Because the Church is predominantly a sacramental community, the Holy Sacraments hold the most important position among all Church actions.

A mystery (sacrament) is a sacred act the bishop or priest administers. Each sacrament has two aspects. The first aspect is the visible, audible, or tangible one. Into this aspect falls the visible means of a sacrament, such as water, oil, crowns, bread, wine—simply all those things we can see or touch during the administration of a sacrament, as well as those things we can hear, such as prayers and chanting.

The second aspect is the invisible one, which is the grace of God bestowed upon the receiver. God's grace is the power of the Holy Spirit granted through the sacrament. This power leads us to spiritual perfection and salvation.

Baptism

THROUGH THE SACRAMENT OF BAPTISM, we are received into the Holy Church, into communion with Christ. We become Christians. This sacrament is regularly administered by a bishop or a priest, irregularly by a layman in case of danger of death, when every minute counts and a priest is not available.

Baptism is administered in the name of the Father, and the Son, and the Holy Spirit, by three immersions in water. With each immersion we die with Christ, and with each bringing up from the water, we are resurrected with Him. Thus we are made new men and women who are not anymore of this world, only living in it.

Jesus Christ established the Sacrament of Baptism by His own example, and again after His glorious Resurrection, when He commanded His disciples to go to the whole world to teach and baptize all nations. Our Lord also clearly indicated that Baptism is absolutely necessary for our salvation.

Baptism can be administered only once; it cannot be repeated. Each candidate for Baptism must have a sponsor (a godfather or godmother). Sponsors must be Orthodox because they have an obligation to help the parents with the upbringing of the new Christian within Orthodoxy. A non-Orthodox person, obviously, cannot accomplish such an obligation.

In some Orthodox jurisdictions, a separate service for the "churching" of the infant and mother takes place forty days after the birth of the child and should precede baptism. This blessing follows the Jewish tradition wherein parents would take their firstborn son to the temple forty days after his birth to be dedicated to God. It involves giving thanks for the safe delivery of the child as well as the mother's return to communal worship. This service also represents the child's first introduction to the Church, prior to baptism. In other jurisdictions, the churching ceremony is done as part of the Sacrament of Baptism and has the same meaning and significance.

In the Orthodox Church, the Sacrament of Baptism is usually followed immediately by the Sacraments of Chrismation and Holy Eucharist, described below, regardless of the age of the recipient.

Chrismation

THE SACRAMENT OF CHRISMATION IS administered in the Orthodox Church immediately following Baptism. Thus these two sacraments form one sacramental rite.

The principal visible aspect of Chrismation is the holy oil, called holy myrrh. The baptized Christian is anointed with this oil on several places on their body with the exclamation: "The seal of the gift of the Holy Spirit."[4] The holy chrism is prepared and blessed exclusively by the bishop, as needed, and then distributed to the priests for

---

4   https://www.oca.org/orthodoxy/the-orthodox-faith/worship/the-sacraments/chrismation.

use in the Sacrament of Chrismation. Converts from non-Orthodox Christian communities, whose baptism the Orthodox Church recognizes as valid, are received into the Church through the Sacrament of Chrismation.

Saint Cyprian excellently explains the meaning of this sacrament: "Those baptized in the Church are sealed by the seal of the Lord after the example of the baptized Samaritans who were received by the Apostles Peter and John through laying on of hands and prayer (Acts 8:14–17) . . . That which was lacking in them, Peter and John accomplished . . . Thus it is also with us. . . . They that are made perfect by the seal of the Lord."[5] The Sacrament of Chrismation comes down to us from the holy apostles. In their time, it had the appearance of laying on of hands.

The Sacraments of Baptism and Chrismation, while distinct, are closely linked. Because we are born anew in baptism, any and all sins are

---

5 Cyprian of Carthage, Epistle 73, "To Jubaianus, Concerning the Baptism of Heretics," in *Ante-Nicene Fathers*, eds. Alexander Roberts and James Donaldson, vol. 5 (Christian Literature Publishing Co., 1886).

forgiven. The further spiritual development of a Christian depends on his or her free will. With the power of the Holy Spirit granted to us in the Sacrament of Chrismation, we have all the help we need to keep undefiled the garment of incorruption we received in baptism.

The Eucharist

THE EUCHARIST IS THE SACRAMENT of Sacraments: the most precious Body and Blood of our Savior Jesus Christ. Not a mere memorial but an incomprehensible reality, it is the true and real Body and Blood of Christ. Jesus established this holy sacrament at the Last Supper, and it is also called the Mystical Supper or the Lord's Supper. At the celebration of the Divine Liturgy, the operation of the Holy Spirit changes the offered Gifts of bread and wine into the Body and Blood of Christ, and believers receive it for the remission of sins and life everlasting, as well as for the healing of the body, mind, and soul.

The Sacrament of the Eucharist is the center of the life of the Church. It is received in full connection with the Faith that makes it impossible for non-Orthodox Christians to commune in the Orthodox Church and for the Orthodox Christian to receive in any non-Orthodox community.

We receive this wonderful sacrament on a regular basis, not just once a year or so, because we need Christ on a regular basis. To receive once a year, as a minimum, is very poor and is a non-sincere formality. Naturally, taking Holy Communion must never become automatic and must always be preceded by preparatory prayers and fasting from midnight. Those who must take medication, perhaps, with some light food, or who have other medical problems that do not allow for a strict fast, will approach the parish pastor and ask for permission to commune. Excuses like, "I cannot go to Holy Communion often, for I am not worthy of it," is just that, an excuse. Of course you are not worthy of it—neither am I, and neither is anyone else. Christ gives Himself to us freely, with compassion and love, and exactly because He knows we are not worthy of it. Let's give Him great thanks! After all, this is what the word *Eucharist* means: "thanksgiving."

Confession

OUR LORD JESUS ESTABLISHED THE Sacrament of Confession after His Resurrection. He breathed upon His disciples, bestowing on them the Holy Spirit, and said to them that whatever sins they remit or retain will be remitted or retained in heaven as well.

Only bishops or priests can administer this holy sacrament. Yet, bishops or priests are merely visible instruments: God Himself invisibly performs the sacrament through them. Like the Eucharist, the Sacrament of Confession should be received regularly.

This holy sacrament has several segments. First, we have to prepare ourselves so that we do not come to the sacrament without knowing what to do or say. There is not even one person who is without sin, so the preparation consists of the examination of our conscience, realizing how we have offended God by what we have thought, said, done, or not done. By all these sins we miss the true target, which is God Himself and His heavenly Kingdom. Second, we confess our sins, clearly and without excusing ourselves, usually in front of an icon of Christ, sometimes with our hands placed on a cross or Gospel book, with the priest standing by our side. Thus, we are actually confessing to God with the priest serving as a witness, trusted advisor, and spiritual father.

Third, at the conclusion we express our sincere sorrow for all our sins and, asking God for help in order to better our life, we ask our father confessor for admonition, penance, and absolution. If the confessor establishes some penance, we perform it as soon as possible. Finally, after we receive absolution we may ask the father confessor for specific advice concerning specific problems. We do not voice or insist on our own opinion but rather listen intensively to what our father confessor has to say.

In his book *Orthodox Dogmatic Theology*, Fr. Pomazansky excellently sums up the Sacrament of Confession: "In the mystery of repentance, the spiritual afflictions of a man are treated, impurities of soul are removed, and a Christian, having received forgiveness of sins, again becomes innocent and sanctified, just as he came out of the waters of Baptism. Therefore, the mystery of repentance is called 'spiritual medicine'."[6]

The Sacraments of Confession and Holy Communion nourish us during our spiritual struggle, enabling us to achieve the baptismal goal, our salvation. Accordingly, we should be receiving these sacraments throughout our lives and on a very regular basis.

The Priesthood (Holy Orders)

THROUGH THE LAYING ON OF hands and specific prayers by the bishop, men who are called to special service in the Holy Church are given divine grace for such service.

These men are called by God Himself. This call appears in the form of a great interest for serving the Church and often develops into an irresistible desire to do so. In the early Church, certain men were recommended or elected for priestly work.

---

[6] Michael Pomazansky, *Orthodox Dogmatic Theology: A Concise Exposition,* trans. Seraphim Rose (St. Herman of Alaska Brotherhood, 1984).

But mere election never made anyone a priest. So, by the hand of the bishop, it is through the call by God and the ordination by God, not by men, that the candidate becomes a priest. Divine grace is granted to the candidate through the hands of a true successor of the holy apostles, the bishop, and it is granted eternally.

The sacred priesthood is threefold: The deaconate is the lowest rank in the priestly order. The deacon has a predominantly liturgical function, but if a bishop or priest requests it, on the parish level he assists the priest in other functions as needed, primarily those oriented to pastoral service such as teaching classes and making hospital visits. The liturgical books of the Church clearly indicate that there is hardly one Church service that can be celebrated without a deacon.

In the absence of a priest, the deacon, with the blessing from the bishop, can serve certain non-sacramental services by himself. Even in such cases the deacon cannot give a blessing, but he can offer prayers and distribute the Holy Eucharist to the faithful *if* the gifts have been consecrated in advance (presanctified).

The deaconate can be a preliminary step to ordination into a higher rank of the priestly orders, or it can be a permanent rank for life. The Church compares the deacon's service to that of the holy angels. Every parish should have deacons. In the early Church, there were also women ordained into the holy deaconate but not to any other priestly order and, in all likelihood, not for liturgical services.

The holy priesthood is a higher order than the deaconate but lower than the episcopacy. Mostly, the priest serves in a parish. He is assigned there only by the diocesan bishop and by him only can the priest be reassigned. The priest is the head of the parish and is the guardian and administrator of the Holy Sacraments. He is also the guardian and teacher of Orthodox Christianity and is a preacher, counselor, liturgist, and visitor to the ill and disabled. In the local church (the parish), the priest represents the bishop, to whom he is fully responsible. The priest is the father to his flock, which he leads with kindness but also with impartiality. The priest is assisted by lay members of a parish board or council, who support him in the non-priestly functions of the parish such as financial management and care of the buildings and grounds.

The holy episcopacy is the highest rank in the priestly order. The bishop is a true successor of the holy apostles. He is the head, the supreme leader of his diocese, with the highest authority. Without his blessing, nothing can happen in the diocese. It is the bishop around whom the Church is gathered, and without him there can be no true Church. He is the guardian and administrator of the Holy Sacraments. He is the archpastor of his diocesan flock, a chief spiritual father to his diocesan clergy and laity. He is the defender of true Orthodox Christianity and a teacher, preacher, and counselor. Only he can ordain deacons, priests, and other clergy, and two or three bishops are required for the consecration of another bishop, as another reminder of the importance of conciliarity in the leadership of the Church.

Bishops cannot be married and are called either from the monastic order or from the ranks of widowed presbyters. Priests and deacons in the Orthodox Church may be married, but they have to receive the Sacrament of Matrimony *before* their ordination to the deaconate. They are not permitted to remarry if their wife dies.

The validity of all the priestly functions does not depend on perfection or the spiritual heights of deacons, priests, and bishops. They surely are expected to adhere to the highest spiritual standards, yet they still have human imperfections. It is God's grace working through them that accomplishes the sanctification and salvation of the faithful.

In addition to the priestly orders, there are two more orders of lesser clergy: readers and subdeacons. There is also a special order that can easily be considered sacramental: the order of monastics. In some Orthodox jurisdictions, blessings may be given by the bishop for chanters, teachers, and other pastoral roles, as needed.

Marriage (Holy Matrimony)

IN THE SACRAMENT OF HOLY Matrimony, a man and a woman are joined, by the grace of the Holy Spirit, in a perpetual union by the bishop or priest.

The family thus formed, especially with the coming of children, is an essential cell not only of secular society but chiefly of the Church. In fact, the family itself is called by the holy apostles a "church."

Very rarely, the Church agrees to permit the dissolving of a marriage—specifically when it is destroyed by adultery or desertion. Generally, the Church does not grant divorces but, out of compassion, tolerates civil divorce. Depending upon the Orthodox jurisdiction, a bishop can grant an ecclesiastical divorce if certain specific conditions are met. Only the diocesan bishop can grant permission for a second marriage in the Church. Permission for a third marriage is rarely granted, and fourth marriages are not permitted by canon law.

The Church does not administer this sacrament if one of the candidates is not Christian. Originally, according to Canon Law, the Church did not administer it if one of them was not an Orthodox Christian, even if both parties were Christians. Nowadays, the Church tolerates so called "mixed marriages" of Orthodox and non-Orthodox

Christians in the hope that the non-Orthodox spouse will, in time, convert to Orthodoxy.

The Orthodox Church does not see marriage as a contract between spouses, where the bishop or priest is only God's witness, as the Western Church does. Additionally, marriage is not only "till death do us part," but forever. That's why a second marriage ceremony has a penitential quality.

This sacrament has several parts, or rites: 1) the rite of betrothal, when the rings are placed on the fingers of the couple; 2) the Sacrament of Marriage, also called the crowning, because by placing the crowns, or flower wreaths, upon the heads of the betrothed and with the blessing, "O Lord our God, crown them with glory and honor"[7] repeated three times, the couple is wed to each other; 3) the drinking from the common cup and the procession three times around the table upon which lays the Book of the Holy Gospels. The groom and the bride have their hands held tightly by the priest's

---

7   https://www.oca.org/files/PDF/Music/Marriage/marriage-service.pdf.

epitrachelion,[8] and the priest leads the procession holding the precious cross in his hand; and 4) the removing of the crowns and the blessing of the newlyweds.

Depending upon the priest's direction, couples about to be married generally receive the Sacrament of Confession. In a mixed marriage, the Orthodox spouse is required to do so and must receive the Sacrament of the Eucharist as well. That's why Sunday is the best day for receiving the Sacrament of Holy Matrimony. There are days when marriage cannot be celebrated, especially during fasting periods. The couple must ask the priest about days on which marriage is permitted and not permitted before planning the date of the wedding. The couple is usually required to attend premarital counseling.

Same-sex marriages are expressly forbidden in the Orthodox Church, in that such unions are

---

8   The epitrachelion (Greek ἐπιτραχήλιον, "around the neck") is the stole worn by Orthodox priests and bishops as a sign of their priesthood. A priest wears the epitrachelion whenever he performs priestly duties.

inconsistent with our beliefs about creation, the nature of human persons, and gender roles. The Orthodox view of marriage is that it is an icon of the relationship between Christ (the Bridegroom) and His Church (the bride).

Additionally, precisely because marriage is a sacrament, it is a holy event sanctified by the Holy Spirit, and any degradation of it to the level of a social affair or a simple show is unthinkable.

Unction (the Sacrament of Healing)

IN ORTHODOX DOGMATIC THEOLOGY, FR. Pomazansky explains this sacrament well: "The Mystery of Unction is a sacred action in which, while the body is anointed with oil, the Grace of God, which heals infirmities of soul and body, is called down upon the sick person. It is performed by a gathering of presbyters, ideally seven in number; however, it can be performed by a lesser number, and even by a single priest." The holy oil is the healing oil blessed by priests during the celebration of this sacrament.

In his letter, the Apostle James gives a clear testimony of this sacrament existing in apostolic times (James 5:14). There, he says that the sick person should call the presbyters of the church, who will anoint them with oil and will pray that the Lord will heal them.

Thus, if anyone in the parish becomes sick, he or she must immediately call the parish pastor and ask for the administration of the Holy Sacraments. If the sick person cannot do this on their own, then a family member calls the priest on their behalf. To call the priest is not optional, but a necessity. True, God works through doctors and nurses, but above all, He works through His Holy Church and heals by the power of the Holy Spirit, granted through the Sacraments.

The Sacrament of Healing is administered to all the sick and suffering and is not reserved just for the dying: There is no such thing in the Orthodox Church as "last rites." To those on their deathbed, this sacrament, of course, can be administered as well, but it is more important for them to receive the Sacraments of Confession and Eucharist before departing from this earthly life.

The Sacrament of Healing is administered on an individual basis to all the sick throughout the year. But once a year, on the evening of Holy and Great Wednesday, it is celebrated as a special service and given to all Orthodox faithful present in the Church, for no one is perfectly healthy, bodily or spiritually.

Finally, the concluding note of this chapter is not so much out of context as it might seem, for along with the Holy Sacraments we are also talking about the parish. We regularly receive the Sacraments of Confession and Holy Communion in the parish where we are members. If we travel and desire to commune in another Orthodox parish, we ask our parish pastor and the pastor where we are visiting for a blessing to do so. We receive the Sacrament of Holy Matrimony in our parish, we baptize our children there, and one day, we will be buried there.

It is precisely this sacramental life that establishes our true membership in the parish. We cannot pay our way into heaven. We must first know where we belong and why. Only then will our financial support of the parish make sense and become, not a burden, but a loving and greatly generous sharing. Only then can we do serious business, spiritual and any other. Such a thing as a "private" Orthodox Christian cannot exist. We belong to the Church, and we must belong to a parish—not only formally but also actively. Every parish represents the whole Church in her fullness and totality.

Once we become members of a parish, we stay there. Changing membership from parish to parish mostly for selfish reasons is most unwise, and it shows a misunderstanding of what the Church is actually all about. We are not members of a church because we like the priest or the deacon. Nor do we leave because things do not go our way, or because someone said or did not say something, or because we dislike the money management, or the singing, and so on. We belong to the Church to glorify God and to save our souls. We must demonstrate our loyalty, stability, and sincerity.

Serious situations might occur that necessitate changing parish membership, such as moving or falling sick and needing to find another, closer parish, and so on. In such cases, it is proper, if possible, to discuss the reasons for the move with the pastor of each parish, as a courtesy to both pastors, as well as for the benefit of one's spiritual health and growth.

CHAPTER 5

The Bible and Holy Tradition

The Bible

THE BIBLE IS THE BODY of sacred writings that record the revelation of God. For this reason, the Bible is also called the Sacred Scriptures or the Word of God. The whole Bible, as we know it today, was written over a very long period of time. God did not write it personally, neither did He dictate it word by word. Rather, we say that the writing of the Bible is "inspired." This means that each writer (and there are a good number of them) was moved to do the writing and then protected from making mistakes by the Holy Spirit Himself. Thus, the Bible is free from mistakes or contravention.

Naturally, we must keep in mind that the Bible is not a scientific book, and therefore there can occasionally be found in it some errors in the fields of astronomy, physics, and so on—that is, in fields that are not important to the message the Bible delivers: God's revelation to us.

The Bible has two basic divisions: the Old Testament and the New Testament. The Old Testament came to us from the Jews—or as they are also called, the Israelites or Hebrews. All the books of the Old Testament were written before the Nativity of Our Lord Jesus. This portion of the Bible contains fifty books, and generally speaking, it deals with God's promise to send the Messiah to the world. Therefore, this is a writing of promise and preparation.

The first five books of the Old Testament are called the Books of Moses, or the Torah. These are Genesis, Exodus, Leviticus, Numbers, and Deuteronomy. There we find the description of God's creation of the cosmos, Adam and Eve's Fall, God's promise of salvation to Abraham, the story of Cain and Abel, and that of Isaac and Jacob. Further, we also read about the liberation of the Israelites from their Egyptian slavery by the Holy Forefather Moses, the travels of the Israelites through the wilderness toward the Promised Land, and Moses' receiving of the Ten Commandments from God on Mount Sinai. These books also contain a large number of moral and ritual laws, and laws concerning the priesthood.

After these five books, there are the Historical Books, followed by the Books of Wisdom, including Psalms, Proverbs, and Song of Songs. There are also twelve books of the Minor Prophets and four of the Major Prophets: Isaiah, Jeremiah, Ezekiel, and Daniel.

The New Testament consists of twenty-seven books. It took several centuries for the Church to decide which books would form the canon of Scripture. There were many other pious and spiritual writings that, for various reasons, were not accepted into the canon of New Testament writings. We call these writings the Apocrypha. These books are considered worthwhile for personal reading and reflection, and may be useful in our Christian education, but they are considered "extra-biblical" in that they are not part of the canon and are therefore not read in liturgical worship.

The first four books of the New Testament are called the Holy Gospels and were written by the four Holy Evangelists Matthew, Mark, the iconographer and physician Luke, and John the Theologian. These books present us with the life and teaching of Christ.

The Holy Gospels, like the other books of the New Testament, were not written by God personally; neither did He dictate them word for word. But similarly to the Old Testament, they were inspired by the Holy Spirit and under His protection are free of any error or controversy when it comes to divine revelation. The Gospels do not contain every minute detail about Christ's life and teaching, since not even all the libraries in the world could hold all the volumes for such a record, as St. John writes in his Gospel. But the writings in these four Gospels are absolutely sufficient for our faith.

After the Holy Gospels comes the Acts of the Holy Apostles, written by the Evangelist Luke. This book describes the first church and the apostles' efforts to spread the teaching of our Lord throughout the world. Following the book of Acts are books of letters, or epistles, of the Apostles Peter, Paul, James the Just, John the Theologian, and Jude. The last book of the New Testament is the Book of Revelation, or Apocalypse. In this book, St. John the Theologian records revelations that God granted him when he was in exile on the Island of Patmos.

All the books of the New Testament are about the fulfillment of the promise God gave to our forefathers. The promised Messiah came: He is our Lord and God and Savior, and His name is Jesus Christ.

Holy Tradition

HOLY TRADITION IS AN ENORMOUSLY large source of Church teaching, spirituality, history, law, iconography, music, liturgical practice, and so on. The first part of Holy Tradition is the Scripture, both the Old and New Testaments. The interpretation of the Bible is not left to the opinions of individuals: The only interpreter of the Word of God is the Church. Another part of Holy Tradition is

Orthodox teaching as presented to us in the writings of the Holy Fathers of the Church and the declarations of the seven ecumenical councils. The third part of Holy Tradition is the teachings of the Orthodox Church, which are not necessarily preserved in writing but were always and everywhere accepted by all, kept and handed down from generation to generation from the time of our Lord Jesus and His apostles.

All these parts of Holy Tradition are equally correct, equally authoritative, and equally binding.

The Seven Ecumenical Councils

THE FIRST ECUMENICAL COUNCIL WAS convened in Nicaea in 325. The first part of the Creed was formulated there, stressing the divinity of the Son of God. The second ecumenical council gathered in Constantinople in 381. The second part of the Creed was formulated there, stressing the divinity of the Holy Spirit.

The third ecumenical council was in session in Ephesus in 431. It defined two truths: Christ is the incarnate Word of God, and the Most Holy Virgin

Mary is truly the Mother of God, the Theotokos. The fourth ecumenical council was assembled in Chalcedon in 451. There, the definition of the two natures of Christ as perfect man and perfect God in one Person was proclaimed.

The fifth ecumenical council was called in Constantinople in 553. The doctrines of the Trinity and of Christ were elaborated and confirmed. The sixth ecumenical council came together in Constantinople in 680. The definition of Christ as truly man, with real human will and actions, was established there. The seventh ecumenical council was held in Nicaea in 787. There, the holy icons were restored to the life of the Church as an integral and inseparable part of Holy Tradition.

Many other decisions, dogmas, definitions, and formulas were established at these ecumenical councils, including the sacred canons of Church law. None of this was mere human creation, fantasy, or elaboration by the Fathers gathered at these councils. It is the Holy Spirit who speaks through them to us, and there is no authority on earth that could cancel even one single decision made at these councils.

CHAPTER 6

The Orthodox Services and Liturgical Cycles

THE RICHNESS OF THE SERVICES of the Orthodox Church corresponds precisely with the richness of Orthodox theology and spirituality. It is well-stated that as we worship, so we believe.

The liturgical services are strictly guided by the time of day and the days of the week, and by the monthly calendar and the yearly cycle. Therefore, we recognize four liturgical cycles on a general basis, and the special paschal cycle of services.

The daily liturgical cycle has a duration of one day, beginning on the evening of the previous day with the Vespers service. It continues with Compline and the Midnight Service. Then follow the liturgical Hours, the morning service called Matins, and the conclusion of the cycle, the Divine Liturgy. If there is no Divine Liturgy, for whatever reason, the typical Psalms (Typika, or in Slavic churches, Obednitsa) are served as a non-sacramental "replacement" for the Liturgy.

In various parishes, usually before great feasts, the services of Vespers, Compline, Midnight, Matins, and Hours are served in one long service called the All-Night Vigil. This is usually abbreviated into a service of Vespers with the Litiya—the blessing of the five loaves, wheat, wine, and oil—and Matins, concluding with the reading of the First Hour.

The fullness of the daily cycle is not usually kept in the parish setting. It is sometimes kept in cathedral churches, where the liturgical life should be exemplary. It is fully served in monasteries.

The weekly liturgical cycle is guided by the days of the week, which means that every day of the week is dedicated to a specific celebration or commemoration. Thus, Sunday is the day of Christ's Resurrection, a "little Pascha," as we say.

Monday belongs to the holy angels, and on Tuesday we remember St. John the Baptist. Wednesday and Friday are days of remembering our Lord's suffering and His death on the Cross. For this reason, we fast on Wednesdays and Fridays every week. Thursday is the day of our Holy Fr. Nicholas the Wonderworker, Bishop of Myra and Lycia, and of the holy apostles. Saturday belongs to the Most Holy Theotokos and Ever-Virgin Mary, together with the holy martyrs and the holy monastic fathers and mothers. Saturday is also traditionally the day for remembering the souls of the departed, although many parishes do serve memorials (Panikhida, Mnemósynon, Parastos) on Sundays at the conclusion of the Divine Liturgy.

The monthly liturgical cycle is guided by the calendar for each month. When we look at our Orthodox calendar, there is not even one day blank—on every day we remember one or more saints or holy events. It is not an overstatement when we say that in the Orthodox Church, every day is a festival. Thus, when the services of the daily cycle are served with the commemoration from the weekly cycle, we add to it a commemoration of a saint or an event falling on that day of the month.

The yearly liturgical cycle is composed of the great feasts of the year—which, of course, repeat themselves yearly—and of the other major feasts of the year. The twelve great feasts belong in this cycle, and they are listed in detail in the next chapter. And there is a thirteenth feast celebrated in every parish with great solemnity, the parish's name day, or the parish feast.

The greatest celebrations of the year come in the paschal season, which has its own cycle, the paschal liturgical cycle. This cycle is divided into several time segments: the pre-Lenten period, or Triodion, Great Lent, Holy Week, The Great and Holy Pascha of the Lord, Bright Week, and the rest of the paschal season until the leave-taking of Pascha, the day before the Ascension of Our Lord.

Most of the feasts of the yearly cycle have fixed dates, in that they are celebrated every year on the same date. Such feasts are called immovable feasts. Other feasts are celebrated depending on the date of Pascha, which changes every year.

Their dates are not firmly fixed, so they are called movable feasts.

Outside of the liturgical cycles, there are numerous services for many different occasions, like the Trisagion for the Departed, the memorial service (see above), a variety of molebens—or services of prayer—that are served for health, for protection during travel, help in any situation, for giving thanks, and so on. There are also blessings of icons and other religious objects, blessings of homes, as well as many other services. Parishioners should make frequent use of these services, usually found in the Book of Needs, asking the priest to serve any of them, and of course they should be present in church when the service is being celebrated.

There are also wonderfully uplifting services called akathists or canons in honor of the Most Holy Theotokos, the holy angels, and various saints of the Church. Other services are celebrated on special occasions, such as the blessing of graves at the cemetery on designated days, the Funeral Service, and others. Additionally, it should be noted that akathists and canons are also appropriate for inclusion in one's personal prayer rule and may be recommended by one's spiritual father.

CHAPTER 7

The Twelve Great Feasts

The Entrance of Our Lord Jesus Christ into Jerusalem (Palm Sunday)

THIS FEAST OPENS THE DOOR of Holy Week, and its date depends on the date of Pascha each year.

Palm Sunday is preceded by Lazarus Saturday, when we celebrate the fourth-day resurrection from the dead of St. Lazarus, the close friend of our Lord, and the brother of Mary and Martha. The Lord Jesus, before numerous witnesses, called St. Lazarus out from the tomb, back to life.

The Entrance of Our Lord Jesus Christ into Jerusalem was indeed a glorious event. Cloaks and branches of palms were thrown to the ground to pave the way as Christ entered the eternal city, exactly the way only the highest potentates were greeted. But the feelings of the cheering crowd were mixed. Some came to greet Jesus as a political leader who would fulfill the dream of the Jews to reestablish Israel above all nations. Others came to satisfy their curiosity, wishing to see the one who could call the dead back to life, for they had heard about Lazarus. And there were the apostles and many other followers of Jesus who were very much worried, remembering Christ's own prophecy about His imminent suffering and death.

But there was also a group of children with pure hearts. These children, inspired by the Holy Spirit, greeted in Christ the one who came to win the greatest victory, the victory over evil, sin, and death. And on this day, together with those children, we cry: "Hosanna to the Son of David! / 'Blessed is He who comes in the name of the LORD!'" (Matt. 21:9). For, with these children, we greet Christ as the Savior, the King of All Creation, to whom belongs maximal glory and honor, for He is God and man, the Pantocrator, the Ruler of All.

For this feast, the church is decorated with branches of palms and other trees, and palms or other plants such as pussy willows (depending on region, climate, and sometimes local ethnic tradition) are blessed by the priest and distributed to the believers. These branches also signify the saving Cross of our Lord, by which the doors of Paradise were reopened to us. For this very reason, the branches are truly a symbol of victory.

The Ascension of Our Lord and Savior Jesus Christ

After His glorious Resurrection, our Lord spent over one month with His disciples. He further instructed them during that time. He also assigned to them the mission of going to all nations, baptizing them, teaching them, and bringing them into His flock. Our Lord also breathed on His disciples, giving them the power of the Holy Spirit to remit or retain sins.

At the end of this time, our Lord took His disciples to the vicinity of Bethany and there, before their very eyes, He ascended into heaven. The holy angels who were present told the disciples that the same Christ would return again at the end of time to judge the living and the dead. Our Lord ascended into heaven with His glorified body, thus remaining the perfect God but also the perfect man.

The Descent of the Holy Spirit (Pentecost Sunday), The Feast of the Most Holy Trinity

ON THE FIFTIETH DAY AFTER His Resurrection, our Lord sent the Holy Spirit down upon His holy apostles and disciples. He manifested Himself in the form of tongues of fire above the head of each man. At that moment they were filled with divine power, courage, and wisdom. In the blinking of an eye, the simple fishermen with limited knowledge and understanding became brilliant theologians and powerful preachers. Thus, the Church established by our Lord came out of hiding and the apostles bravely faced the task of teaching the nations about Christ the Savior and about the only God who is to be worshipped and who exists in the Holy Trinity. Since that day, when thousands accepted the true Faith, the Church grew, and it continues to grow today.

On this feast, immediately after Divine Liturgy the Vespers of Pentecost is celebrated. During Vespers, the priest recites three long prayers while facing the people, who are all kneeling for the first time since before Pascha. We ask for the divine help of the Holy Spirit and pray for all our brothers and sisters, living and departed.

On this day, some Orthodox churches practice a custom of decorating the church with green branches and/or flowers, which symbolize the perpetual youth of the Church of Christ. In some parishes, the faithful make wreaths of flowers, which are then blessed and taken home.

The Nativity of the Most Holy Theotokos

THIS FEAST IS CELEBRATED ON September 8.

The story of the Nativity of the Most Blessed Virgin is not narrated in any of the books of the Old or New Testaments. It comes to us from an apocryphal writing called the Protoevangelium of

James, dated approximately from the beginning of the second century.

In this book, the author points out that the Most Holy Theotokos was born only after Ss. Joachim and Anna prayed fervently over a long period of time, because St. Anna could not conceive. Finally, God granted them a girl who would soon become the Mother of God. She was named Mary.

The Western Church connects the "immaculate conception" to this event. By this they mean that the Theotokos was born without "original sin," and thus she is unique in this among all of humankind. But the Eastern Orthodox Church always adheres to the original teaching of the Church concerning the conception and birth of the Most Holy Virgin. We teach that it is theologically impossible to inherit the guilt of someone's personal sin and thus inherit the sin of anyone else. Therefore, there is not one person ever born with so-called "original sin," or any other sin, for that matter. What we all inherit is the evil outcome of Adam and Eve's personal sin: a twisted nature, an inclination to evil, a tendency to leave God's path, accepting willingly the sinful way of life, suffering, sickness, and death. And with this and into this outcome, everyone, without exception, is born.

Nevertheless, the Most Holy Theotokos cooperated with the grace of God with perfection, keeping her soul and heart beautifully pure and guarding her virginity as well. For this alone, we may, quite correctly, call her "immaculate."

The Universal Exaltation (Elevation) of the Life-Giving Cross

THIS FEAST IS CELEBRATED ON September 14.

Saint Helen, the mother of Emperor Constantine, on her pilgrimage to the Holy Land, discovered three crosses in the vicinity of Golgotha. Because there was no way of knowing which of the three was the Cross of our Lord, Bishop Makarios decided to test them. When a terminally ill woman touched the first two crosses, nothing happened. At the moment she touched the third Cross, her health and vitality were immediately and perfectly restored, for the third of the crosses was the true Cross of our Lord. Crowds gathered to see this most wonderful tool of our salvation. In order for everyone to be able to see the Cross, Bishop Makarios lifted it up before the crowd of the faithful, so all could venerate it.

But it is the glorious Resurrection of our Lord Jesus that elevates the precious Cross to the attention of the whole world and presents it to humankind as the symbol of eternal life and the key to the gates of Paradise. On this day, parishioners richly decorate the Cross of our Lord, and the priest places it ceremonially on the analogion for veneration. In the Greek tradition, a bed of basil commemorating the finding of the true Cross is used as a decoration, and sprigs of the plant are distributed to the people.

The Entrance (Presentation) of the Theotokos into the Temple

THIS FEAST IS CELEBRATED ON November 21.

Based on apocryphal texts, we know that the Most Holy Theotokos entered the temple at the age of three, accompanied by her parents, Ss. Joachim and Anna, and preceded in a procession by a number of virgins carrying lamps. The reason for her entrance into the temple was for her consecration to the service of God and for her education.

To the amazement of all those present, the soon-to-be Mother of God immediately ascended the steps to the Holy of Holies, the portion of the temple where only the high priest was permitted to enter. She remained there for a very long time in contemplation, being served and fed by the holy angels. It is said that she remained in the temple for a number of years and left shortly before the Annunciation to her by the Archangel Gabriel.

How wonderfully appropriate that the Temple of God, which the Virgin Mary was about to become by bearing the Son of God, entered the temple of the very same God, remaining there in preparation for her motherhood of divine origin.

The Nativity According to the Flesh of Our Lord and God and Savior Jesus Christ

THIS FEAST IS CELEBRATED ON December 25.

In the early Church, the date of this feast varied from region to region. The date that all now keep,

December 25, was established relatively late. But it is not the date that establishes the importance of this feast, it is the fact that God Himself came to us, became one of us, suffered and died, and rose from the dead for us and for our salvation.

As Christ's Crucifixion cannot be considered separately from the Resurrection and vice-versa, so our Lord's Nativity is closely connected with His death. He was born to die for us. On the icon of the Lord's Nativity, his "cradle" is depicted in the form of a tomb.

This magnificent feast is not for shedding sentimental tears over a helpless baby, because this baby is the King of all Creation, God Himself. Also, any type of commercialization has no place in this festivity. And above all, this celebration cannot push Christ out of the picture by replacing Him with Santa Claus. This feast is only about Christ our Lord. Orthodox Christian parents must understand this absolutely clearly.

On the second day of the feast, we honor the Most Holy Theotokos. We cannot do otherwise, for from her, by the power of the Holy Spirit, our Lord and Savior was born. The third day is dedicated to the protomartyr and archdeacon Stephen. He was the first martyr and gave his life for the very same Christ who was born and died for our salvation.

The fourth day of the feast is dedicated to the remembrance of the thousands of holy martyrs burned in Nicomedia. The fifth day celebrates the twenty thousand innocent infant boys killed by the order of King Herod in hopes that one of them would be Jesus.

When we gather around the decorated Christmas tree, which symbolizes the living and lifegiving, victorious Cross of the Lord, let us give thanks to Christ, who lowered Himself in order that we may ascend. Who was born and died and rose from the dead so that we, too, may live.

The Theophany (Epiphany) of Our Lord Jesus Christ

THIS FEAST IS CELEBRATED ON January 6.

This feast is all about the Trinity revealing itself to us. That is the meaning of the word *epiphany*, or *theophany*: the revelation of God. The festal icon is called the "Trinity of the New Testament."

God the Father reveals Himself in the form of a voice from above; God the Son stands in the River Jordan, humbly receiving the baptism of St. John; and God the Holy Spirit descends in the form of a dove.

This feast is also named the Baptism of Christ. The baptism of St. John the Baptizer was that of repentance, but our Lord is perfect—there is nothing within Him He has to repent for. So why did He receive this type of baptism? He did so on our behalf. As He took the Cross upon His divine shoulder, so He took our sins upon Himself, and when he entered the River Jordan, He accepted for us the baptism of repentance. As He said to the reluctant St. John, this had to happen in order to fulfill the Scriptures.

During this feast, the Great Blessing of Waters takes place. The priest, dipping the hand cross into the basin of water, sings the troparion of the feast. Then he and all the people drink the holy water, are sprinkled with it, and take some home to drink in times of sickness. Often, larger bodies of water—rivers, lakes, creeks, and ponds—are blessed on this feast. The priest also goes to parishioners' houses and blesses the dwellings and the inhabitants.

The Meeting (Presentation) of Our Lord in the Temple

THIS FEAST IS CELEBRATED ON February 2.

The Law of Moses required that on the fortieth day after birth, the infant be brought to the temple and an offering presented—usually a spotless lamb—though poor people were permitted to offer two doves or two young pigeons. This is the historical background of the feast.

The theological meaning of this feast is in the word *meeting*. But who, actually, was our Lord meeting in the temple? He was meeting His people: all of us.

In the righteous Simeon, our Lord met all those who recognize Him as the Savior of the world. In the righteous prophetess Anna, He met all who dedicate their entire lives to His service. In the rest of the servants in the temple, Jesus met all those who are still in doubt and spiritual turmoil. In His Holy Mother, who stood at His side, our Savior met all those who say "yes" to God's call and, accepting it, never look back. In His foster father, the righteous Joseph, who accompanied Him, Jesus Christ met all those who, in a heroic way, keep their faith regardless of the odds and humbly accept their place according to God's will. In all these, our Lord met with the whole of humankind.

The Annunciation of the Most Holy Theotokos

THIS FEAST IS CELEBRATED ON March 25, during Great Lent, exactly nine months before the Nativity of Christ. It is one of the earliest Christian feasts, dating back to at least the fourth century.

After the Virgin had been betrothed to Joseph and he had taken her into his home, the Archangel Gabriel appeared to her with a message that God had chosen her to be the bearer of His Son, the Lord Jesus Christ. Through the power of the Holy Spirit, the Virgin would bear a child who would be the "Son of the Most High" and who would preside over a Kingdom having no end. This encounter between the Archangel Gabriel and the Virgin is described in the first chapter of St. Luke's Gospel (vv. 26–38).

In his akathist hymn to the Theotokos, the renowned hymnographer St. Romanos the Melodist (reposed around AD 556) describes the profound sense of wonder the Archangel Gabriel experienced at the mystery of the Incarnation: "The Archangel was sent from Heaven to cry 'Rejoice!' to the Theotokos. And beholding You, O Lord, taking bodily form, he stood in awe" (Eikos 1). While delivering the message of God to the Most Holy Virgin, the angel marveled at the miracle of God actually choosing to dwell in a human womb beyond human logic.

The amazing dialogue between the Most Holy Virgin and Archangel Gabriel, as St. Luke describes it in his Gospel, culminates with the Theotokos's answer: "Let it be to me according to your word" (Luke 1:38). Her humble but definite "yes" put the salvation of the world into motion. For, at that very moment, the Holy Spirit filled the Mother of God with His power, and she conceived the Savior of the whole universe.

We honor the Theotokos as the true Mother of God, and we admire her for her great faith, humility, and courage. She truly is more honorable than the cherubim and more glorious than the seraphim.

The Transfiguration of Our Lord Jesus Christ

ON AUGUST 6, WE CELEBRATE Christ's Transfiguration on Mount Tabor.

There, our Lord showed Himself in His splendid divine nature to the three disciples He took with Him. Christ's appearance became so bright and brilliant that the disciples had to cover their faces. Seeing our Lord in His divine splendor, conversing with the Prophet Elias and Moses, Peter, James, and John were so overwhelmed with the beauty and magnificence of the sight that they did not wish to return to the world down the mountain and suggested to the Lord that they should stay and make their dwelling there. But our Lord returned to His human appearance. The disciples could not exactly comprehend what had happened and, if they could not understand it, the rest of humankind could not either. That was why our Lord requested that they keep this event secret until after His Resurrection.

This feast stresses the two natures of Christ: the human nature, which the disciples saw in Him on a daily basis, and His divine nature, which He revealed to them on the mountain.

Because this is also harvest season, we bring the first fruits of our labors to God as an offering on this feast. The priest blesses the grapes and other fruit, asking God to bless those who will partake of them and praising God for His generosity.

The Falling Asleep (Dormition) of the Most Holy Theotokos

THIS FEAST IS CELEBRATED ON August 15.

Apocryphal texts narrate to us that all the holy apostles, except St. Thomas, were miraculously transferred from all the corners of the world to the deathbed of the Mother of God. Christ Himself received her holy soul and carried it to heaven. With great piety, the holy apostles placed the body of the Most Holy Mother of God into the tomb.

There was an incident on their way to the tomb. A man approached the dead body of the Virgin with the intention of insulting it. At the moment he stretched out his hand to overturn her bier, an angel cut it off with a sword. The man repented and this time touched the body with great reverence and admiration. Immediately his hand was restored to perfect health.

On the third day, the Apostle Thomas arrived, having been delayed for some reason. He insisted on seeing the body of the Theotokos, so he could pay his last respects. When the apostles opened the tomb, it was empty. Then the apostles realized that Christ had assumed not only the soul but also the body of His Holy Mother into heaven. For this reason, this feast is also called the Assumption.

In some Orthodox traditions, it is customary to bless flowering herbs or flowers on this day, which remind us of the beautiful scent of fresh flowers coming out of the tomb of the Most Holy Theotokos. Some parishes also prepare a decorated tomb, similar, but smaller than that prepared for Christ on Great Friday. The icon of the Dormition of the Theotokos, in the form of a shroud, is carried in a procession, placed in the tomb, and venerated.

Major Feasts

IN ADDITION TO THE TWELVE great feasts, there are a good number of major feasts, some of which are also celebrated in the parishes.

September 1: The Church New Year
September 24: The Holy Martyrs of Alaska: St. Peter the Aleut and St. Juvenaly
October 1: The Protection of the Most Holy Theotokos
October 6: The Glorification of the Holy Hierarch Innocent
October 26: St. Demetrios the Myrrh-Gusher
November 8: Synaxis of the Holy Archangel Michael and the Other Bodiless Powers of Heaven
November 30: St. Andrew the Apostle
December 6: St. Bishop Nicholas, Wonderworker
December 13: Repose of Holy Fr. Herman of Alaska, Wonderworker

January 1: The Circumcision of Our Lord; the Commemoration of St. Basil

January 7: St. John the Baptist

January 30: The Three Holy Hierarchs (St. Basil the Great, St. John Chrysostom, St. Gregory the Theologian)

March 31: The Repose of the Holy Hierarch Innocent, Apostle to the Americas

May 11: The Holy Equals of the Apostles, Cyril and Methodius

May 21: Ss. Constantine and Helen, Equals to the Apostles

June 24: The Nativity of the Holy Prophet, Forerunner, and Baptist John

June 29: The Holy Apostles Peter and Paul

July 20: The Holy Prophet Elias

August 1: The Procession of the Precious Cross of Our Lord

August 9: The Glorification of Holy Fr. Herman of Alaska, Wonderworker

August 29: The Martyrdom of the Holy Prophet, Forerunner, and Baptist John

CHAPTER 8

The Paschal Liturgical Cycle

THE PASCHAL CELEBRATIONS ARE THE greatest feasts among all feasts. They are beautiful and quite numerous. These celebrations are not only at Holy Pascha itself but encompass quite a long period of time before and after Pascha as well.

We start with the time of preparation. This season encompasses the three weeks before Great Lent. The Sundays of these weeks are 1) the Sunday of the Publican and Pharisee, of which the main theme is humility, as the first aspect of true repentance; 2) the Sunday of the Prodigal Son, of which the main theme is our return to the Father; 3) the Sunday of the Last Judgment, also called

Meatfare Sunday, on which we commemorate all the holy ascetics and fasters as our guides and examples in the spiritual ascent; we also start a limited fast, abstaining from meat; and 4) the Sunday of Forgiveness, also called Cheesefare Sunday, of which the main theme is forgiveness. At Forgiveness Vespers, often served immediately after Divine Liturgy, we ask forgiveness of each other and we also forgive everyone, for how could we otherwise expect our heavenly Father to forgive us. This is the last day before Great Lent, and we put aside all meat, dairy products, and eggs until Pascha.

Great Lent starts on the Monday after Cheesefare Sunday. Its length is six weeks, or forty days. It ends on the Friday evening before Palm Sunday.

Great Lent has special liturgical characteristics. The first of them is the Great Canon of St. Andrew of Crete, in which we contemplate the history of salvation through the Old and New Testaments. This is then applied to the situation of the sinful soul. Another special characteristic is the use of the Prayer of St. Ephrem the Syrian. This prayer is recited very often during Great Lent and is accompanied with prostrations. The beauty and inner power of this prayer are so important for spiritual growth that it should also be prayed privately at any time during the whole year:

> O Lord and Master of my life, take from me the spirit of sloth, despair, lust of power, and idle talk. But give rather the spirit of chastity, humility, patience, and love to Thy servant. Yea, O Lord and King, grant me to see my own transgressions, and not to judge my brother, for blessed art Thou, unto ages of ages. Amen.[9]

During Great Lent, it is typical to use readings from the Old Testament in the daily liturgical cycle, specifically readings from Genesis, Proverbs, and the Prophecy of Isaiah. Also, a specific liturgical book called the Triodion is used, which contains special Lenten texts and hymns.

---

9   https://www.oca.org/orthodoxy/prayers/lenten-prayer-of-st.-ephrem.

The typical Liturgy on weekdays of Great Lent is the Liturgy of the Presanctified Gifts, served on Wednesdays and/or Fridays in most parishes.

On the first four Fridays of Great Lent, many parishes read a portion of the Akathist Hymn to the Most Holy Theotokos, with the entire Akathist read on the fifth Friday.

On the Sundays of Great Lent, the Divine Liturgy of St. Basil the Great is celebrated. These Sundays, besides keeping their Sunday resurrectional character, each have a specific theme:

- The first Sunday is dedicated to the commemoration of the Triumph of Orthodoxy over iconoclasm. At this time, a special Vespers service that includes a procession of icons and the recitation of the Synodikon (a statement of Orthodox beliefs originating from the Seventh Ecumenical Council) takes place. This council is credited with the restoration of icons to Orthodox churches and homes in AD 787.
- The second Sunday is dedicated to the memory of St. Gregory Palamas, who taught about deification in Christ.

- The third Sunday is that of the Veneration of the Precious Cross, in which a beautifully decorated cross is placed in the center of the church and venerated by the faithful. In some parishes, flowers from the cross are distributed to the faithful at the conclusion of the Sunday Liturgy.
- The fourth Sunday is dedicated to the memory of St. John of the Ladder, the ascetic author of *The Ladder of Divine Ascent*.
- The fifth Sunday is dedicated to our Holy Mother Mary of Egypt, an ascetic and perhaps the most outstanding example (icon) of whole-life repentance.

The first Saturday of Great Lent is dedicated to the Holy Martyr Theodore the Recruit. The remaining Lenten Saturdays are dedicated to the commemoration of the departed, until the fifth Saturday, which is dedicated to the *Akathist to the Theotokos*.

All Lenten Saturdays and Sundays are days of eucharistic celebration. We already know that Lenten weekdays celebrate the Liturgy of the Presanctified Gifts. During the week, vestments are of a dark color, melodies are of a solemn Lenten melody, and the prayer of St. Ephrem is used. Saturdays and Sundays are different because the vestments are of a light color, the Lenten melody is not used, and St. Ephrem's prayer is omitted. Even though the order of services is not of the Lenten type on Saturdays and Sundays, fasting continues.

During Great Lent, we make an effort to participate in the services and receive Holy Communion as often as possible. We also make our lenten holy Confession, which is not the only confession we make in the year, of course, but is an integral part of the Lenten spirit of repentance. It will greatly assist us in our true repentance, for we all know that repentance is nothing less than an unshakable change of mind, and therefore a change in our way of life, and an enthusiastic yet humble return to God the Father. Great Lent leads us to reevaluate our priorities and reorganize our scale of values by giving us the most wonderful tools to use: prayer, fasting, good deeds, the Holy Sacraments, church services, intensive reading of the Gospels and of the lives of the saints, and so on. These are the Lenten activities that also make fasting meaningful; otherwise, it would be nothing else but senseless human dieting.

Holy Week starts on the Monday after Palm Sunday. All the days of Holy Week are called "Great and Holy," and they all start with Matins, served, by anticipation, on the previous evening.

The Matins of the first three days of Holy Week are called Bridegroom Matins, and they are served in the evening before each of these three Holy Days. The main theme corresponds with the name of the services: Christ our God, the Bridegroom, comes. He loves us and expects us to love Him.

On Great and Holy Monday and Tuesday, the last Liturgies of the Presanctified Gifts are served. On Great and Holy Wednesday, the Sacrament of Holy Unction or the Sacrament of Healing is celebrated in the evening. At the end of that service, all those present are anointed with healing oil, which the priest blessed during the service. On Great and Holy Thursday, we remember the Last Supper of our Lord. During the Vesperal Liturgy of St. Basil, a supply of the sacrament for use throughout the year is prepared and reserved for communing the sick and disabled who cannot come to church.

Great and Holy Friday is a day of mourning, for on this day our Lord died for our salvation on the Cross. The Matins for this day is sung on the evening of Great and Holy Thursday. The central focus of this Matins service is the reading of selections from the twelve Holy Gospels that are related to the Passion of our Lord.

On the morning of Great and Holy Friday, the only day of the year when no Liturgy may be served, the Royal Hours are served, which again retell the story of our Lord's Holy Passion. In the afternoon, the Vespers of the Crucifixion is served, a powerful service featuring a reenactment of the taking down (sometimes referred to as "the unnailing") of Christ's body from the Cross and his burial in the Tomb. Later, on Friday evening, the Matins of Holy Saturday are served, during which the shroud of Christ (winding sheet, *plaschanitsa*, or epitaphion) is processed three times around the outside of the church. Later, the shroud is placed into the flowery tomb for veneration, and the night watch is kept at the tomb. Also, the Lamentations of the Theotokos are chanted.

On the morning of Great and Holy Saturday, the Vesperal Divine Liturgy of St. Basil the Great is celebrated, including multiple readings from the Old Testament. Because this is the day of anticipation of Christ's Resurrection, the altar coverings and vestments are changed from purple to white.

The greatest of all feasts, the feast of feasts, the glorious Pascha of the Lord, is all about His Resurrection. Our Lord, out of His own divine power, rose from the dead on the third day.

There are strict rules for the calculation of the date of Pascha. The Orthodox Church celebrates Christ's holy Resurrection on the first Sunday after the full moon coming on or immediately after March 21. The full moon here is not the astronomical full moon but is established according to ancient ecclesiastical computation. Also, according to the declaration of the Ecumenical Council of Nicaea in 325, the Pascha of our Lord must never precede or coincide with the Jewish Passover but must always follow it. Because the

Western Church disregards this binding decision of the Council of Nicaea, the dates of Pascha for the Western Church and the Orthodox Church are rarely the same.

The Paschal or Resurrection Services of the Orthodox Church are typically celebrated at midnight, beginning with a brief Midnight Office that actually begins late Saturday. At the conclusion of the Midnight Office, all the lights in the church are extinguished, and the priest, carrying a large lit paschal candle, emerges from the altar and declares that Christ is resurrected. From this candle, other candles held by the faithful are now lit.

The priest, carrying the paschal candle, leads the congregation in a procession (which varies according to tradition) during which the hymn "Thy Resurrection, O Christ Our Savior" is sung continuously. Upon arrival at the main doors of the church, the Resurrection account from the Gospel of Mark may be read, and the paschal troparion "Christ is risen from the dead" is sung. The priest and congregation reenter the church, which has now been fully illuminated. This beautiful sight inspires intense joy and a sense of otherworldliness amongst the faithful.

Paschal Matins is then served, followed immediately by the Divine Liturgy with special paschal characteristics. For example, the paschal troparion "Christ is risen" is sung again and again, and the Gospel is often read in multiple languages. In lieu of the usual sermon, the priest instead reads the Paschal Homily of St. John Chrysostom.

At the conclusion of the Liturgy, it is customary to distribute colored eggs (usually red) to the faithful. In some traditions, people bring baskets of special paschal foods to the services to be blessed. The baskets generally contain all the foods from which the faithful abstained during Great Lent.

The Paschal Vespers service takes place during the day of Pascha (Sunday). The time can vary based on parish tradition.

The week following Pascha is called Bright or Renewal Week. The Divine Liturgy of St. John Chrysostom, following the same order as on Pascha, is celebrated each day of the week.

The first Sunday after Pascha is known as Antipascha and is also known as St. Thomas's Sunday.

In some traditions it is customary to visit cemeteries to bless the graves of the faithful. This might also occur on a different day, such as the Tuesday after St. Thomas's Sunday. As the priest blesses the graves with holy water, exclaiming "Christ is risen," the paschal troparion is sung.

The paschal cycle continues with special commemorations of various saints and events from the Gospels on each of the Sundays. The Wednesday before the Feast of the Ascension is the leave-taking of Pascha, ending the paschal celebration for the year.

Even though we recognize the paschal season liturgically as a finite, fifty-day cycle, we should remember that every Sunday Divine Liturgy is a commemoration of Christ's glorious Resurrection—a little Pascha—and that this is also why we do not kneel on Sundays.

CHAPTER 9

The Orthodox Divine Liturgies

IN THE ORTHODOX CHURCH, WE celebrate several types of the Divine Liturgy. This is the main divine service of the Church, the bloodless sacrifice, the Holy Eucharist. If the Divine Liturgy is celebrated by a bishop, it is called hierarchical.

Before the beginning of the Divine Liturgy, the priest prepares the gifts of bread—called prosphora, made of leavened dough and wine, and mixed with water—at the table of oblation in the sanctuary. This service is called the Proskomedia. It is a service of preparation and oblation of the gifts that will be changed during the Divine Liturgy, by the power of the Holy Spirit, into the true Body and Blood of our Savior Jesus Christ.

The Divine Liturgy cannot be served on behalf of one person as it can be in the Western Church. The priest commemorates individuals, living and departed, by their names at the Proskomedia service, removing a particle of bread for each name and placing it on the diskos; after this, these particles are placed into the chalice. Individuals are also prayed for during the Liturgy, but the Divine Liturgy is always celebrated "on behalf of all, and for all."[10] For this reason, there is no Requiem Mass served in the Orthodox Church. If there is a funeral service connected to the Divine Liturgy (for example, at the funeral of a priest or bishop), then the Liturgy is celebrated with the texts of the day, and the Litany for the Departed is added just before the Litany of the Catechumens—but it is not a Liturgy for the Departed. The liturgical service for the departed is called Panikhida and it is a nonsacramental service.

The Divine Liturgy has two parts. First is the Liturgy of the Catechumens, which is concluded by the dismissal of the catechumens before the Creed is spoken. The second part is the Liturgy of

---

10 https://www.oca.org/orthodoxy/the-orthodox-faith/worship/the-divine-liturgy/the-divine-liturgy.

the Faithful, from the Prayers of the Faithful to the Dismissal.

The Liturgy of the Catechumens is divided into the Synaxis (or gathering together), which contains the Great Litany, three antiphons, the Little Entrance, and the Trisagion. Then comes the Liturgy of the Word with the epistle and Gospel readings and the sermon.

The Liturgy of the Faithful, from which the catechumens are dismissed, continues after the prayers of the faithful with the Great Entrance, when the Gifts are ceremonially transferred from the proskomedia to the holy altar. Then follow the Litany and Kiss of Peace, the Creed, and the Anaphora, when the Gifts are changed by the Holy Spirit into the real Body and Blood of Christ. Next is the Hymn to the Theotokos, the Litany and the Lord's Prayer, the Communion Hymn, and the Communion of the Holy Gifts by the clergy and the people of God. The Liturgy concludes with the Litany of Thanksgiving, the Prayer before the Ambo, and the Dismissal.

Everyone should come to the celebration on time but definitely not later than the reading of the Holy Gospel, assuming one has a serious and valid excuse for appearing late. Similarly, one should stay until the very end of the Liturgy and come forward to venerate the precious Cross in the priest's hand. Unfortunately, there are always those who adopt the bad habit of habitually showing up late for the Liturgy and/or "hiding" in the vestibule rather than coming into the nave for the entirety of the service. Here again, unless one has a valid excuse such as needing to calm a crying child, such behavior is irreverent and must be avoided.

THE DIVINE LITURGY OF ST. JOHN CHRYSOSTOM is celebrated most times of the year, on Sundays and feast days, and is structured in the form we all know, bearing the name of our Holy Fr. John Chrysostom.

THE DIVINE LITURGY OF ST. BASIL THE GREAT was formulated by the saint whose name it bears. This Divine Liturgy is celebrated on the Sundays of Great Lent, on the Feast of St. Basil, Christmas Eve, Epiphany Eve, Holy Thursday, and Holy Saturday.

The Liturgy of St. Basil does not differ in structure from the Liturgy of St. John Chrysostom, but it has some different and longer texts, notably in the Prayers for the Catechumens and of the Faithful, and the Anaphora, which is very long but beautiful, and the prayers before and after the Lord's Prayer.

THE DIVINE LITURGY OF ST. JAMES was formulated by the Bishop of Jerusalem whose name it bears. This liturgy is practically forgotten, and is celebrated only on the Feast of St. James and on the Sunday of the Holy Righteous Ones, which is the Sunday after the Nativity.

The Liturgy is extremely beautiful and is the oldest Liturgy in Christianity. Saint James died about AD 70; it is therefore assumed that he wrote his Liturgy before then and that it was used as the Eucharistic worship service for the church.

THE DIVINE LITURGY OF THE PRESANCTIFIED GIFTS was formulated by St. Gregory Dialogos and is very old. Saint Gregory was the pope of Rome in times when the popes still adhered to Orthodoxy.

This liturgy is specifically celebrated during Great Lent in the afternoon or early evening because it has the character of Vespers combined with the addition of Holy Communion. During Great Lent, it is not permitted to celebrate the Divine Liturgy of Ss. John Chrysostom or Basil the Great on weekdays, because those Liturgies have a resurrectional character that clashes with the topic and mood of Great Lent, and so they are celebrated only on Saturdays and Sundays during Lent. But in order to give the people of God the opportunity to receive the Holy Eucharist on weekdays, the Divine Liturgy of the Presanctified Gifts is celebrated on every Wednesday and Friday of Great Lent.

During the Sunday Divine Liturgy, the priest prepares two extra Lambs,[11] which he treats exactly the same way as the Lamb for the Sunday Liturgy, with the exception that he places them into a special container after he dips them into the Blood of our Lord in the chalice. The container, box, or pix stays on the altar, and the Lambs, which are presanctified (that is, they are the true

---

11   The center of the prosphora that is transformed into Christ's Body.

Body of our Lord dipped into His true Blood), are left to dry there and then are distributed to the faithful at the celebration of the Presanctified Liturgy. Before Holy Communion, the priest cuts the dried Lamb into small pieces that he places in the chalice with wine to be softened.

If we wish to simplify the explanation of the structure of the Liturgy of the Presanctified Gifts, we might say that it is actually Vespers with Holy Communion, where there is no Anaphora. It starts like the regular Divine Liturgy, but it enters into the structure of Vespers immediately after its beginning. Then it returns to the structure of Divine Liturgy.

In this Liturgy, the Great Entrance is made in silence, the priest transferring the Presanctified Gifts from the table of oblation to the holy altar while the people make a prostration. Holy Communion is distributed as usual.

After every Divine Liturgy in which we receive Holy Communion, we should be reading the prayers of thanksgiving. In some parishes, a reader chants these prayers at the conclusion of the Liturgy. Those attending parishes where this is not done should read these prayers at home. After all, we thank someone for giving us even a small gift; this is considered good manners. How much more essential it is to thank the almighty God for granting us the greatest possible gift, communion with Himself!

CHAPTER 10

Fasting and Praying

IN THE ORTHODOX CHURCH, WE fast often. If we were to sum up all the Wednesdays and Fridays and add the other fasting periods, we would see that we fast almost half the year. What is so important about fasting? It is an integral part of the spiritual ascent of every Orthodox Christian. We do not see fasting as merit-generating, as does the Western Church. They, of course, have their point. If fasting for them is the fulfillment of a requirement, then obedience is definitely a merit-giving virtue.

But for Orthodox Christians, fasting is not the final goal in itself. Rather, it is a tool, an exercise, a way to train. As athletes must train and exercise, as virtuoso musicians must constantly practice their instruments, so Orthodox Christians need to fast. The fast liberates us from excessive attention we would normally pay to worldly affairs. The point of fasting is not what we give up but rather what we bring in. Since the bringing in is of a spiritual character, there is naturally less space for material things. Thus, fasting must necessarily be accompanied with prayer, good works, spiritual reading (especially from the Bible, the lives of the saints, and other Orthodox literature), receiving the Holy Sacraments, faithfully attending church services, and making an effort to live our lives in a way that is pleasing to the Lord. If this is missing, then our fasting is nothing more than dieting, and it has nothing in common with spiritual growth.

First of all, we fast every Wednesday and Friday throughout the whole year. There are some exceptions—the fast-free weeks indicated in the calendar.

Fasting is also required on several single days: the eve of Theophany (January 5), the Martyrdom or Beheading of St. John the Baptist (August 29), and the Elevation of the Precious Cross (September 14). There are also entire seasons of fasting during the year: the Nativity Fast, also called St. Philip's Fast (from November 15 through December 24); Meatfare-Cheesefare-Great Lent (determined according to the date of Pascha each year); the Apostles' Fast, also called Ss. Peter and Paul Fast (from the Monday after All-Saints Sunday through the eve of the Feast of Ss. Peter and Paul); and the Dormition Fast (from August 1 through August 14).

There are guidelines for fasting that come to us from deep history, and often they are quite strict. The strictest way of fasting is kept in monasteries and by ascetically inclined people, and it is certainly a wonderful thing to be able to fast in that way. But for those faithful in the parishes who must regularly go to jobs that often demand physical exertion, the strictest rules of fasting need not apply.

The first rule must always prevail: Do not disregard the fast. The second rule is that we adjust our way of fasting in such a manner that we will be able to keep it faithfully and regularly throughout the whole season. In other words, do not try to be a hero by setting strict rules for yourself but then abandoning them the next day.

The third rule is that we eat no meat at all, throughout the whole fast. The fourth rule is that we drink no alcohol, for it clouds the mind and leads us to abandon the spiritual way of life. The fifth rule is that we eat no dairy products. The sixth rule is that, strictly speaking, fish is not a fasting food, even though it may have become so on the parish level. The seventh rule is to lessen the number of meals during the day when we fast: It is not a bad idea to skip either breakfast or lunch. And even the most innocent snacks between meals should be eliminated. The eighth rule is to take truly small portions of everything. The ninth rule is to remember that the spiritual life must accompany fasting. The tenth rule is that we smile, for we do this fasting for the glory of God and for our salvation. Fasting is not a torture but is the training of the spiritual athlete. If you cannot live up to all of these rules, then at least set some rules for yourself and keep them.

Fasting rules and guidelines can vary by jurisdiction and individual parish. Each person must ultimately decide how, and to what extent, he or she can faithfully keep the fast. One can consult one of the many church calendars or, for more individualized guidance, consult one's parish priest or spiritual father. Even if one is not able to keep a very strict fast for health or family reasons, it is still advisable to limit one's intake of food as much as possible, possibly by eating smaller meals, limiting portion sizes, and eliminating snacks.

Typically, various forms of entertainments and parties are discouraged during fasting periods, especially the Great Fast. Our intention should be to keep our minds firmly on spiritual matters. Fasting is serious, and we should take it seriously, but not in such a way that we become legalistic or pharisaical about it.

Finally, we must never judge the fasting (or lack of fasting) of another person. It is important to remember that fasting is done for the benefit of our spiritual development.

It is definitely not harmful to introduce children to the ways of fasting, setting for them a milder rule. This will go with them for the rest of their life. Naturally, they also learn from the example given by their parents. Very mild rules, if any, apply to the elderly. Those who are ill or who have an exact therapeutic diet set for them by a doctor or other healing practitioner can disregard fasting concerning food, but not the spiritual side of fasting. Always seek the advice of your pastor, if in doubt. You might be surprised at how simply your problems may be solved and your questions answered.

Another mighty tool, the true ladder of ascent, is prayer. The power of prayer is astonishingly great.

There is a common misconception about prayer among Orthodox Christians: Even very pious people are under the impression that real prayer must be lengthy. But actually, the length of the prayer has nothing to do with its effectiveness. To recite pages of prayers from the prayer book does not necessarily mean that we are really praying.

To conclude, let's listen carefully to what St. Theophan the Recluse has to say about prayer:

"Prayer is the test of everything; prayer is also the source of everything; prayer is the driving force of everything; prayer is also the director of everything. If prayer is right, everything is right. For prayer will not allow anything to go wrong."[12] And elsewhere, this Holy Father says:

> Without inner spiritual prayer there is no prayer at all.... What then is prayer? Prayer is the raising of the mind and heart to God in praise and thanksgiving to Him and in supplication for the good things that we need, both spiritual and physical. The essence of prayer is therefore the spiritual lifting of the heart towards God.... Outward prayer alone is not enough.... Feeling towards God—even without words—is a prayer. Words support and sometimes deepen the feeling.[13]

---

12 St. Theophan the Recluse in *The Art of Prayer: An Orthodox Anthology*, compiled by Igumen Chariton of Valamo, trans. E. Kadloubovsky and E. M. Palmer (Faber and Faber, 1966), 53.

13 Theophan, *Art of Prayer*, 53, 54, 60.

And in yet another place, he says:

Which is better: to pray with the lips or with the mind? The answer is that we must use both forms: pray something in words, sometimes with the mind . . . It is better to put it this way: Pray sometimes with sounding words, and sometimes inaudibly with words that are soundless. But it is necessary to take care that both sounding and soundless prayer should come from the heart. . . . To pray is quite straightforward. Stand with the mind in the heart before the face of the Lord and cry: 'Jesus Christ, Son of God, have mercy upon me' or just: 'Lord, have mercy,' 'Most merciful Lord, have mercy upon me, a sinner'—or with any other words. The power is not in the words, but in thoughts and feelings . . . The principal thing is to stand with the mind in the heart before God, and to go on standing before Him unceasingly, day and night, until the end of life.[14]

---

14 Theophan, 62–63.

CHAPTER 11

The Trisagion Prayers

THIS IS A COMPOSITE PRAYER that is used as a beginning at almost all Orthodox Christian services. We should all know this prayer by heart. It also makes an excellent short daily prayer rule to be prayed in the morning and in the evening.

We start by making the sign of the holy cross and saying:

In the Name of the Father, and of the Son, and of the Holy Spirit. Amen.

Glory to Thee, our God, glory to Thee.

O Heavenly King, the Comforter, the Spirit of Truth, Who art everywhere and fillest all things; Treasury of Blessings, and Giver of Life—come and abide in us, and cleanse us from every impurity, and save our souls, O Good One.

Holy God! Holy Mighty! Holy Immortal! Have mercy on us. (3x)

Glory to the Father, and to the Son, and to the Holy Spirit, now and ever and unto ages of ages. Amen.

O Most Holy Trinity, have mercy on us. O Lord, cleanse us from our sins. O Master, pardon our transgressions. O Holy One, visit and heal our infirmities, for Thy name's sake.

Lord, have mercy. (3x)

Glory to the Father, and to the Son, and to the Holy Spirit, now and ever and unto ages of ages. Amen.

Our Father, Who art in Heaven, hallowed be Thy Name. Thy Kingdom come; Thy will be done, on earth as it is in Heaven. Give us this day our daily bread; and forgive us our trespasses, as we forgive those who trespass against us; and lead us not into temptation, but deliver us from evil.

Lord, have mercy. (12 x)

Glory to the Father, and to the Son, and to the Holy Spirit, now and ever and unto ages of ages. Amen.[15]

---

15   https://www.oca.org/orthodoxy/prayers/trisagion.

About the Author

FATHER PAVEL SOUCEK WAS BORN on December 10, 1939, in Prague, Czechoslovakia, to Vaclav and Jaroslava Stara Soucek. From an early age he showed remarkable academic and artistic promise, laying the foundation for the priest, scholar, and artist he would later become.

In 1957, once he had finished secondary school he enrolled at Charles University in Prague, studying Roman Catholic theology. His schooling was disrupted when Communist authorities barred him from continuing, but he eventually finished his degree in 1969, adding mathematics and computer programming to his studies. He briefly worked at the Biophysical Institute of the Medical Faculty of Charles University, and around that time he married (Matushka) Paula Novakova (of blessed memory). In 1969, the couple and their first son emigrated to the United States, seeking the freedom and opportunity denied to them under the Communist regime.

Once in New York City, Fr. Pavel resumed his theological path, enrolling at the General Theological Seminary and being ordained to the Episcopal priesthood in 1974. His spiritual journey led him through the Lutheran and Anglican Catholic traditions and ultimately to the Orthodox Church, where he found the fullness of the faith he had long sought. In 1980 he and his family entered the Orthodox Church, and he then continued his formal theological studies at Saint Vladimir's Orthodox Theological Seminary in Crestwood, New York. There, on Bright Saturday, May 2, 1981, he was ordained to the holy priesthood by Metropolitan Theodosius.

Father Pavel went on to serve in numerous dioceses of the Orthodox Church in America,

About the Author

including New England, Western Pennsylvania, the South, and the Midwest. His parish assignments included Holy Trinity in Willimantic, Connecticut; St. Michael's in Irvona, Pennsylvania; Nativity of the Theotokos in Madera, Pennsylvania; Ss. Peter and Paul in Miami, Florida; and Holy Assumption in Marblehead, Ohio, from which he retired. His priestly ministry was marked by his clarity of teaching and a pastoral attentiveness rooted in compassion and wisdom. He was elevated to archpriest and then protopresbyter in 1992, and granted the right to wear the palitza in 2004.

A lifelong scholar, Fr. Pavel earned multiple graduate degrees, holding master's degrees in theology, divinity, science, and herbology. He was also a certified gerontologist and later completed a doctorate in philosophy. His intellectual talents were matched by remarkable artistic and musical gifts. A skilled iconographer and prolific painter, his work adorns homes and churches throughout the United States and Europe, each piece reflecting deep theological insight and artistic refinement. As a composer of both secular and liturgical music, he contributed richly to the cultural and spiritual life of every community he served. He was also a master musician, proficient on several instruments.

In addition to his scholarship, artistry, and pastoral work, Fr. Pavel was a man of wide-ranging interests whose personal library, creative output, and multilingual abilities reflected a mind always seeking truth. Those who knew him remember his kindness, his keen sense of humor, and his ability to meet people with warmth and understanding.

After retiring in 2005, Fr. Pavel continued to create, study, and support the Church he loved. On Thursday, January 15, 2009, he fell asleep in the Lord. His legacy endures in the hearts of his parishioners, his family, and countless others touched by his life and ministry.

For Further Reading

All of these books can be purchased at the Ancient Faith Store, https://store.ancientfaith.com/.

The Ancient Faith Prayer Book, ed. Vassilios Papavassiliou (Ancient Faith Publishing, 2014).

Come, Let Us Worship: A Practical Guide to the Divine Liturgy for Orthodox Laity, V. Rev. Patrick B. O'Grady (Ancient Faith Publishing, 2016).

How to Read the Holy Fathers: A Guide for Orthodox Christians, Fr. Joseph Lucas (Ancient Faith Publishing, 2025).

Introducing the Orthodox Faith: Its Faith and Life, Fr. Anthony Coniaris (Light & Life Publishing, 2010).

An Introduction to God: Encountering the Divine in Orthodox Christianity, Fr. Andrew Stephen Damick (Ancient Faith Publishing, 2014)

Journey to Reality: Sacramental Life in a Secular Age, Zachary Porcu (Ancient Faith Publishing, 2024).

Know the Faith: A Handbook for Orthodox Christians and Inquirers, Fr. Michael Shanbour (Ancient Faith Publishing, 2016).

The Orthodox Way, Bishop Kallistos Ware (SVS Press, 2019).

Thinking Orthodox: Understanding and Acquiring the Orthodox Christian Mind, Dr. Eugenia Scarvelis Constantinou (Ancient Faith Publishing, 2020).

We hope you have enjoyed and benefited from this book. Your financial support makes it possible to continue our nonprofit ministry both in print and online. Because the proceeds from our book sales only partially cover the costs of operating **Ancient Faith Publishing** and **Ancient Faith Radio**, we greatly appreciate the generosity of our readers and listeners. Donations are tax deductible and can be made at **www.ancientfaith.com.**

To view our other publications,
please visit our website:
store.ancientfaith.com

Bringing you Orthodox Christian music,
readings, prayers, teaching, and podcasts
24 hours a day since 2004 at
www.ancientfaith.com

www.ingramcontent.com/pod-product-compliance
Lightning Source LLC
LaVergne TN
LVHW040102080526
838202LV00045B/3738